# NOTES
## OF A
# JEWISH
## CONVERT
## TO THE
# LDS
# CHURCH

*Conversion of a Soul*

## MARLENA TANYA MUCHNICK

Seattle, Washington
Portland, Oregon
Denver, Colorado
Vancouver, B.C.
Scottsdale, Arizona

Layout & Production: Matt Westfield
Cover Design: Dave Marty


Cataloguing in Publication Data
Muchnick, Marlena Tanya


Notes of a Jewish Convert to the LDS Church:
Conversion of a Soul

ISBN 0-89716-803-8
LOC 97-075942


First Printing January 1998

Peanut Butter Publishing
Pier 55, Suite 301
1101 Alaskan Way
Seattle, WA 98101-2982
206/748-0345, Fax 206/748-0343
e-mail: pnutpub@aol.com • http://www.pbpublishing.com
Vancouver B.C. • 604/688-0320   Portland • 503/222-5527
Denver • 303/322-0065    Phoenix/Scottsdale • 602/947-3575


Printed in the United States of America

# Table of Contents

# Dedication

This book is devoted to the development of understanding and empathy between two major ideologies: Judaism, and the full Gospel of our Savior and Messiah, as taught in The Church of Jesus Christ of Latter-day Saints. I fervently hope my experiences and testimony will help to bring about an enduring fraternity between the two religions.

# Acknowledgements

I owe so much to Karen and Andy of Junction City, Oregon, who shared with me the full Gospel of Christ as taught by The Church of Jesus Christ of Latter-day Saints. Without their devoted friendshipping, their guidance and love, this book would never have been written. I know the Lord directed me to them that I might find the eternal keys to the salvation of my soul.

I also wish to thank my brother, Mark, who was the first in our family to become a Mormon. It was he who planted the first tenuous seed.

Many thanks to Sister Anita Hallock of the Springfield, Oregon Second ward. A talented author in her own right, Sister Hallock diligently edited this manuscript and helped me to focus my thoughts. She somehow understood immediately my deep need to write it. Her ideas enlivened the text, added necessary highlights and helped me to focus on the true thematic content. I know we were prompted to work together.

I am especially grateful to Sister Glenda Perryman of the Brenham, Texas branch. Glenda has a fearless missionary spirit. Without her great enthusiasm, her awesome editing skills and her generosity in guaranteeing that this book be published, it would probably be consigned finally to the archives of my closet. Glenda is my great friend and I am fortunate beyond expression.

# Song Of Inspiration

My Father, whom I love so dear,
Thou art my Light, my shining hour.
Beneath Thy just, refining Hand
My blessings multiply.

As Thou reveals Thy will, Thy Law -
This student lists on bended knee,
With quickened ear and grateful heart.
And knows that Thou art God of all.

O bring me joy and whisper nigh
Thy secrets of eternity
That I may hear Thy deepest thoughts,
That truth may ever burn in me.

O loose me not, my precious Lord
For I, Thy child am evermore
Thy servant, Thy disciple suffering long.
But bless me as the Saints of old:
Smart and brave and Gospel strong

That I may more fully serve Thee
on high
In this waste place,
Then later in Thy courts of peace.

O, how I love Thee, Father.
Father, how I love Thy Son.
Who ransomed me from death and from
The awful sins of flesh

That I might come forth to see Thee,
To dwell forever in Thy light.


Marlena Tanya Muchnick

# Preface

When a Church sister asked me to plan a Passover *seder* for her family I was moved to think she cared enough about the Jews to wonder how they worshipped God and expressed their love through a traditional dinner celebration. We shared that Passover experience on a Family Home Evening in their home several months before I joined the LDS church. They were impressed by the level of tradition and symbolic ritual that goes into the preparation and experiencing of that most important Jewish holiday.

I realized how little she or her husband knew about the Jewish religion and culture, and how hungry they were for that knowledge.

Were other members of the Church equally curious? Would they enjoy participating in the Jewish experience? Could exposure to Jewish thought and culture enrich Mormon life? Could it contribute to brotherly love? Would it help them as they studied the Old Testament, New Testament, Pearl of Great Price, The Book of Mormon?

I found the answer to all those questions is a positive one. Jesus was a Jew. His perfect life, the manner in which he died and his resurrection were a sign to all of us that we are a united people. Our separate beliefs, once understood, once respected, will reinforce that unity. Then we can be worthy brothers and sisters to all we meet.

I believe it to also be true that exposure to the Gospel Jesus preached will, without fail, enrich the lives of all Jews who truly seek to know God. His only Begotten Son was himself a Jewish man who came to speak first to his own people. They mistook him for a simple teacher and rejected him. It is prophecy that gentiles will eventually teach the Jewish people everywhere the true Gospel of Jesus Christ.

Because I am a Jew who has wholeheartedly embraced the Gospel according to The Church of Jesus Christ of Latter-day Saints, I can testify as to how both cultures have enriched my life. Though I no longer celebrate Jewish holidays or ceremonies, the memories I have remain forever in my heart and consciousness.

Though I have embraced Christianity, my precious Jewish heritage has been retained and I hope this little book will be a good way to share it with you.

I am no less a Jew but more fully God's servant.

*L'chaim!* To life and health!

Marlena Tanya Muchnick
alias *Menucha Toiba*
(peaceful reader of scripture)
Seattle, Washington
1997

# Chapter One

What Am I Doing Here?

1.

I know it was the burning desire for an unshakable belief in God which drew me, after many lonely years, to the Junction City, Oregon ward chapel of The Church of Jesus Christ of Latter-day Saints one clear winter day in 1988. I was scared and uneasy at my first sacrament meeting as an investigator. I thought guiltily of the *rabbi* at the synagogue I had been attending across town. If he should see me here he would shake his head, throw up his hands and pray for my return. But everyone I met this special morning in church was kind to me and solicitous. Eventually I calmed down and became engrossed in the service.

My good friend Betty introduced me to the bishop of the ward at that first sacrament meeting. I remember his asking if I had ever seen a temple.

"Oh, yes," I answered vigorously. "I've attended lots of them over the years." I hoped he'd be pleased.

"Which ones," the bishop asked, his eyes widening with interest. "Salt Lake? Seattle?"

"Oh, no. I haven't made it there yet. But I went to *Beth Sholom* and *Beth Eretz* and *Beth--*." I stopped. The bishop really looked confused now. "Where?" he asked. "I've never heard of those wards."

Suddenly I understood his confusion and felt really foolish. "Bishop, please forgive me. Those are Jewish temple names (interchangeable with synagogue). I'm Jewish. I'm here to investigate the Church."

This time his smile was beautific. With one strong arm he gave me a bear hug. "Well, well. Welcome to church." Then he winked and said "We've been expecting you."

It's taken me a while to figure out what he meant by that, but I know now he knew the Spirit had brought me home. That was a great day for me, because it had taken nearly all of my life before the fruits of my search for spiritual truth could at last be tasted.

2.

Being raised Jewish is somewhat a sensual experience. Suddenly I can see my grandmother's chicken soup boiling with rice and onions, bright orange carrots tossing in the pot. The smell is enticing, the grease forming cobwebs on the water. Later when the soup cooled that grease would congeal and be scraped away. I will never forget the wonderful acidic aroma of that soup and of the *gefilte* fish (*matzoh* meal and whitefish) shaped into balls or patties, which we often ate with *borscht* (beet soup) or other hot or cold soups.

I remember, too, the thrill of going with my parents to the Farmer's Market in Los Angeles, that unique bazaar of foods smack in the heart of the city, full of exotic delicacies from around the world. We always headed first for the prickly green kosher pickle barrel. My dad would tell us to stick our arms down into it and pull up a giant pimply green pickle, succulent and salty. Oh, boy! When I was young, one of those could last me a long time. I always tried to get as many as my hands could hold!

But there is food for the body and food for the soul. With a greater reverence I recall the touch of so many objects in the synagogue; my Star of David, small and gold plated, with sharp corners that I used to scratch the back of my hand to form another star. The old prayer books with their fine, smooth pages that turned so quickly to the center of the volume that I could never find the right prayers in time. How clumsy the book felt in my hands because all books containing Hebrew prayer and scripture open on the right side and are read from the back of the book to the front. I remember the cool feel of the prayer shawl (*talis*) hanging in a closet near the meeting room, waiting for the *rabbi* and his *minyan* - a group of ten men over thirteen years old (not unlike a quorum) to don them and the *yarmulkes* (skullcaps) preparatory to beginning services.

And I will never forget the sweet/tart taste of the Sabbath wine - Mogen David grape. Until many years later Mogen David was the only wine I tasted. I did not like it. It startled me, reminding me that it was hard to be a Jew and to drink bitter wine, eat *matzoh* and try to learn Hebrew and Yiddish.

Being at a Jewish prayer service is an especially sense-related experience. The gutteral noises in the word *baruch*, the sweet poetic sound of *adonai,* a word for the Holy One. I love the throat clearing syllables in the word *elohenu* (king). Jewish prayer is a process that involves the entire throat, lungs and mouth -- even, *oy vay*, the sinuses!

And the beautiful dances!  The joyous wedding dances, the food, the humor, the prayers, the bride's tears and the groom's face glowing with pride.  I will always cherish those memories.  I will always hear the songs of praise and joy, often sung in minor keys with many flats, sung often in the form of a wail heavenward, a serenade of love for our Eternal One's pleasure.

3.

A Jew lives a very secular life style, often sensing him or herself an outsider, a member of a special interest group, a part of the Judean desert history, if you will.  Being raised Jewish means, among so many other things, that a belief in Jesus as the Messiah is antithetical to the concept of monotheism.  Judaism is essentially a belief in one God without Christ or a defined Holy Spirit.  It is in many ways a religion of history in which the Jewish national state, past and present, plays an urgent part.  When I was growing up we did not go searching for friends among those of other religions.  My parents cautioned me against this, saying I could not affiliate with *goyim* (non Jews).  For the most part I heeded their instructions.

I do recall meeting a few Mormons while I was growing up, but, dutiful to my mother's urgings I was never friendly with them.  The few times I heard about Mormons I was told only that the men could have more than one wife if they chose, and that their beliefs were based upon an obscure book made of gold and found in a forest by a child.  I was cautioned that they were weird and wouldn't let any outsiders join their church.  Strangest of all, I was told by my Jewish friends that they considered themselves descendents of the tribes of Israel, fancying themselves to be actual Jews.

I was intrigued by that information and amused.  I wondered why those people went to so much trouble to construct a heritage of such complexity when all they had to do was to realize they could never be Jews because a true Jew is born of a Jewish mother.  Having a Jewish father helps, but the matriarchal line of birth is essential.  We are not of a race of people, but a sub-civilization, a culture complete with all facets: language, theology, a society, specific mores, a secular history, a territory, and much more.  The ancient lineage of a Jew stems from the Judean city where the Hebrews lived.  It was a long time before I understood that Mormons considered themselves Hebrews and did not really understand the difference between being Hebrew and Judaism.  (I have tried to explain the essential differences in the Glossary.)

There is the problem of one God.  To a Jew there has always been only one God, all knowing yet still unknowable.  How could any other religion or culture know the *angst* of a Jew for his persecuted brethren?  Surely they were misled and misinformed. From my ignorant, biased standpoint, never having seen a volume of The Book of Mormon, I dismissed Mormons as a group of Christian come-latelies.

My mother always encouraged me to have Jewish friends, but I remember a family of Irish Catholics I was very fond of as a teenager. Several times I accompanied Carol to her morning mass, our heads draped in black scarves. I listened to those scriptures and songs being intoned in Latin, indecipherable to me. I felt awe and confusion during those liturgies, knowing God must have been listening, too, and wondering how many languages He spoke. I must admit to feeling smug about being one of the "chosen."

We used to discuss how it was, my being Jewish and her being a Catholic; confessing our sins before God, Carol to her priest behind a closed door and myself in *schul* (synagogue), intoning Hebrew prayers. Even then I remember wondering very secretly what it might be like to believe in a Christ; to have a sure knowledge of him, to speak Hebrew to this man who so many millions considered to be a Jew, the Son of my beloved God.

But my parents kept a strict eye on me, nevertheless. They were quite critical and protective of their only daughter and saw to it that I attended temple classes on time so I could become confirmed (graduated) from Sunday school with a working knowledge of Hebrew, competent in the *Torah* and the *Talmud*, familiar with the ritual prayers.

4.

During the early years in Los Angeles, where we moved from Ohio when I was about four years old, the population was about to explode across the landscape. Strangers came from every direction. Freeways went up, tract homes were built and sold like popcorn. Thousands of them became available in only a few years and we eventually moved into one in nearby San Fernando Valley. We all felt smug and casual beneath those mellow skies, basking on weekends along those endlessly warm Southern California beaches.

There were not many synagogues in the valley then. The ones I attended were spare, elongated rooms with partitions, hard metal chairs and hastily built pulpits where the Eternal Light (God is always with us) could always be seen to hang on a cord above the *Torah* scrolls. Many congregation members were also new in our area, from the east and the northeast, looking to set new roots in a newly settled valley of sunshine.

Since only a portion of synagogue attending Jews still tithed a full ten percent, the membership fees to join the congregation were high. The Building Fund was new and bravely dedicated to the eventual erection of a permanent, impressive synagogue with maybe a school, a well-paid *rabbi* and a *cantor* (singer) with an inspiring voice.

## 5.

I would like to report also that I came from a typical Jewish family, but that was not the case. Of course, there are problems in every family, but as Jews my parents were encouraged to keep counsel with the *rabbi* of our local synagogue. He could hear their problems, offering help and guidance. But my father was a very proud man who always believed he could shoulder all responsibility and endure all pain by working harder and longer hours, spending little time with his family and physically disciplining his two children whenever he felt it necessary.

Though my parents were honest, hard working people who usually went to *schul* on Friday nights and to High Holy Day services, our family unit was not a strong one. My father, a contractor, was away for eighteen hours a day, laying tile and linoleum floors, hanging venetian blinds, haggling over carpet prices, driving all over the valley doing jobs. He was the hardest working man I have ever known. At night when he came home he was much too tired to do anything but eat and go to bed. He did take us for drives on Sundays if he didn't work, but there was never time for affection. We were expected to get all of that from Mother, I guess, because Dad never found time for us in that way.

He did counsel us about our activities, impatiently giving directions and commands, showing us the error of our ways over and over until he became disgusted with us. He didn't seem to need or to want our love, but I know he depended upon us to be there to receive him and to be grateful he was providing for us. I adored my father despite his harsh treatment. To this day I have the greatest respect for his memory, as painful as his punishments were, as frightened as I was of his anger. I know he was being fair to us in the only way he knew how.

I learned basic housecleaning and cooking from my mother, who was more home oriented. When I was six, she began to teach me to cook the old fashioned Russian Jewish way which she had learned from her mother. I will always remember making *kasha* (buckwheat groats) and sweet and sour meatballs topped with applesauce and beets. I made *borscht* (beet soup), *challah* (braided egg bread) and *strudel* (filled pastries). At age seven I learned to cook and by the time I was twelve I was a real *baleboosteh* (a homemaker). Just give me a *tisheleh* (table) and a *benkelah* (bench) and I will serve my meat balls to the *goyim* (non-Jews) of the world! I made *latkes* (potato pancakes) and *blintzes* (pancakes wrapped around a filling) and that eternal Jewish standby, chicken soup!

When I was fourteen, my mother began attending U.C.L.A. to become a nurse. I was in charge of the house. I cooked the meals for my dad and for my brother who was seven by that time. He, my only sibling, was disinterested in the goings on at home, but loved to cook. In succeeding years he became an excellent chef.

My mother must have been loving and compassionate to her patients, I am sure, for she often brought home everyone's problems and we'd all mourn together. "*Oy vay*," the saying goes. Oh, pain, pain of life, of death, of protest. "He had no *sachel* (saykhel or common sense). "Well, *nu*, what did you expect?" Then the slow shrug of the neck and shoulders and upturned palms. "God willing, he should be okay." "*Nu* (noo - a sigh or frown, maybe a grin or grunt). *Nu*, so go know he would argue with me!"

We certainly didn't have a household like our neighbors. Anyone opening our door at a given moment would be likely to hear Yiddish or Russian, some German and, rarely, a quote from the Bible in Hebrew. In school I learned French fluently. We spoke a lot of English, too, but peppered heavily with European words.

6.

My brother and I had the distinction of being the only first generation European Jews on the block. My father's family, the Muchnicks (meaning confectioner, baker) were from a small town called Berdichev in the southwestern portion of the Russian Ukraine, below White Russia and just north of the Black Sea. Generations of Muchnicks were raised and schooled there. My mother's folks had come to America from Minsk and Kiev, but I have never been able to locate the exact area or to do their genealogy. Dad was born in Berdichev and naturalized years later in Ohio. He had a number of brothers and sisters, some of whom stayed in Russia when he left in 1914, near the start of the Bolshevik Revolution. That's about when Mom's father and mother, Israel and Esther, left Minsk. Israel had studied in the Russian *shtehtls* to become a *rabbi*. However, once in America he abandoned the idea for lack of money and a need for immediate work, which he found as a floor polisher and janitor of sorts.

Once in America, everyone split up and went their different ways. I have cousins in many states whom I have never seen. Some changed their names, others changed the spellings. This, too, was common for European immigrants in the early years of the century after passing through customs. My dad's family arrived on Ellis Island in l914 and headed straight for Canton, Ohio, to be with relatives also newly there. My mom's parents headed for Cleveland, and my parents met there in l939.

My people were commoners in America, never aspiring to office or becoming rich, but in Russia several of them were judges and held offices of honor. Several more were successful businessmen and raised large families. My father's father, Label, owned a very successful haberdashery in Canton for many years. His name is still known in that city.

No one in my family has ever been in trouble with the law or challenged their government, though our Constitution guarantees us that right. I know they were so proud of becoming Americans and being able to hope for a better life and then to be allowed to work at what they could to achieve a measure of security. No one in my family mentioned to me (or to each other) any homesickness for Russia.

Many nights I remember my grandfather Simkovitz poring over history books and manuals which told about American government, Social Security and the like. But he had lots of interesting stories of life in Russia, having left there an adult. My grandmother held onto her past, however quietly. She alone of my relatives never learned to speak English, though she could understand it well enough. She conversed in Russian or Yiddish or pidgin English, but many times during the day I'd hear her sing Russian lullabies to herself, moving her stout body from side to side in accompaniment.

My ears became used to several languages in those early days. My grandparents spoke Russian, Yiddish and Hebrew. Yiddish is essentially a German dialect which flourished in the *shtehtls* -- the Jewish communities in Western and Eastern Europe before World War II. There in the ghettos Hebrew, German and remnants of the French and Italian languages became mixed together until the Poles, Ukranians, Rumanians and Hungarians evolved the distinctive street language which endures today even among modern Jews as a hallmark of the People Israel.

7.

Judaism is a religion of history, an awareness of the presence of God in human events. We celebrate that relationship throughout our lives. Yiddish is not Hebrew. The Hebrew language, ancient, liturgical and therefore static is used mainly for the performance of religious rites and for reading the scriptures, though in Israel it is the national language and has developed dialects as well as many new words and phrases. Adopted words of many other languages now fit into its lexicon. Hebrew is derived from ancient Aramaic and Persian scripts. In Hebrew Sunday school classes the children who will later become confirmed in their studies will learn to read, write and to sing in ancient Hebrew because all Jewish prayer was, until modern times, conducted in the ancient tongue - an enduring reminder to Jews of their heritage from Jerusalem and beyond, and of their essential tribalness: the past brought into the present on the tongues of the people.

If the Jews are the People of the Book, then the Hebrew language with all its strange script and mystical meanings is our constant reminder of the Book itself.

When my parents divorced in 1954, our family was separated forever from any meaningful life together. I think that is why my brother and I were never really encouraged to study and to prepare for *bas/bar mitzvah*, the traditional ceremonies of adulthood in Jewish life. A young man of thirteen is *bar mitzhvah*ed and the girl receives a *bas mitzvah* to acknowledge her becoming a young woman. It is a refined initiation rite into adulthood and spiritual preparedness. By that time it is expected that Jewish children of twelve to fourteen years of age will have undergone rigorous training in the *Torah* and the *Talmud*, which contains expositions upon the *Torah*. We would have learned fluent Hebrew, Mosaic law and custom, and acquired a readiness for the responsibilities of man/womanhood.

The boy at his *bar mitzvah* becomes committed to lifelong spiritual and ethical obligation. For a girl to become a daughter of the commandments the ceremony is the same, but often held in groups, secondary to the *bar mitzvah* because Judaism is based upon a patriarchal tradition. The male bears the covenant. His birth always brings the greater celebration, as he will someday come to lead his family.

He is now a "son of Israel". *Zy gesundt* (good luck). The parties after the ceremony are always remembered as some of the happiest a Jew can know. The happy graduate gets *gelt* (money gift) from many admirers and, of course, their blessings. All the *kibitzers* (talkers, gossipers) come out to the party and wish the graduate *mazel tov* (congratulations) and say, look how smart he is, how he has grown, may he be so successful in life, *kineahora* (kin ahorra). This is a saying intended to ward off the evil eye, the bad spirits, and to thank God for His grace.

Though I was not *bas mitzvah*ed, I was confirmed from Sunday School in a special service. My parents were duly proud of me, but I recall even then feeling as though I was lacking something.  I recall that even with the learning of Hebrew, knowing the major laws of *Talmudic* teachings, hearing the Sabbath services on Friday nights, I was acutely aware of an uneasiness about my own level of commitment to Judaism.  So I didn't honor the promises I made to continue my study of *Torah*.

### 8.

By this time my personal life had changed for the worse, first because of the new stresses my parents were feeling and second, because of my senstivity to new home arrangements.  I was unhappy that I rarely saw my father.  Also, my mother was finding life increasingly stressful because of her new responsibility as a single parent.  As soon as I became a senior in high school I got a job in a donut shop and contributed to the family income.

After high school I enrolled at the local junior college to study journalism, but changed to an English major to work toward a teaching degree.  My mother, my brother and I sometimes went to Friday night services but were too poor to pay the membership fees.  Eventually, we only went to temple on Jewish holidays, more a token appearance than a real desire to visit the house of God.

### 9.

*To Good Fortune:  May it come up and sprout forth like a green garden.  Whoso finds a great good obtains favor of the good Lord, who ratifies this union.*
*From a Tenaim (Marriage Agreement)*

Divorce in Jewish life is regarded with sadness.  We are instructed to choose valorous Jewish parents.  Perhaps we are even predestined to find these partners for the purpose of making a family.  A home that is filled with love is like a sanctuary, but a loveless home is against the teachings of God, and divorce will be preferred to continuing an unhappy, unfruitful union, though reconciliation is always to be desired.  Children raised in an unhappy home where parents do not love each other, where they fight and abuse one another, are themselves abused, living lives as victims.

My parents were not married by a *rabbi*, but civilly, and they did not live intimately according to Jewish law.  They were orthodox, conservative and then reform (See Glossary), never taking advantage of the advice and guidance the temple programs offered.  Failure to be married by a *rabbi* and to live according to Jewish law and custom effectively means the couple does not wish to live within Jewish tradition or to seek God's blessings as a part of the congregation.  They are not practicing their faithfulness or sharing their spiritual strength with one another.  Such a marriage honors no tradition and sets no example for success.  If it should end in divorce neither partner can expect to find happiness and contentment waiting.  If a Jew does not seek God's blessings, attend synagogue services and Holy day services, he or she lives in denial of God's desire to see His children living together as families in happiness.

That is what happened to my parents.  Eventually the marriage ended and we children were taken from our father to live with our mother.  A way of life ended forever, though we were never better off after that.  My father felt he had worked all those years for nothing, and my mother felt newly vulnerable.  A single parent supporting two youngsters as yet unable to provide her with much support of any kind, living in a time when being a single parent could be a dangerous financial enterprise at best.  Because I had no example to follow I began to invite apostasy into my own life, living without direction, seeking worldly goods and physical pleasures.  When I think of the past and how I wandered so far away from God's blessings I grow sad.  How deeply I needed to know I was a child of the Lord, loved by him.

Before I studied to become a member of the LDS church I had never heard of having a "testimony."  I cannot conceive of a Jewish person bearing a testimony of God or of the *Torah*, and yet I suppose that is what we do in synagogue during all our prayers and rituals.  A devout Jew prays and sings with great passion, and that is testimony enough.  Being raised in the Jewish traditions is itself such a special and different way of life that just to live it well is testimony that we would have chosen to be Jewish, and that we are thankful to God for His mercy toward us.

I can see now that to have a testimony of the truth of a religion is a powerful, self-affirming tool which requires one to ponder and to decide what is believed in and to what extent.  If my parents had developed personal testimonies even as members of a congregation where guidance and wisdom are always in supply, I am sure they would not have created the unhappiness we all had to bear.  Just as having and bearing a testimony of belief in the Lord and our love for him humbles us, we are also reminding ourselves of our willingness to allow the Lord to work in our lives on our behalf through promptings and revelations and through those who are sent to help us progress.  This gift my parents never knew they could have, and how we all suffered for the loss.

10.

As the years passed I educated myself and set some goals for a career.  There were problems with my choices of what would really interest me on a long term basis.  I found myself without a firm idea of what I really wanted to do with my life. I had many unfulfilling jobs, some very good ones and others which I really felt had no future to offer. Eventually I finished my schooling and began teaching. I was estranged from my parents during most of this time. My mother remarried and moved away. Dad was angry with us all for so many reasons, valid and imagined. He refused even to visit with my brother or myself most of the time. My brother had moved from the area, as I had, to forget all the hardships of our childhoods and to make his own life happy.

I had several very unhappy relationships in my youth which added more emotional pain than anything else. I believe these short liaisons were to me ways of finding some affection, filling up the loneliness of being single while all my friends were marrying and having children. I married late, at age thirty. Sol was descended from a family of French Jews. He knew little of their history, but he had a recent personal history full of tragedy. A widower, he and his two lovely daughters had to cope with the death of their mother, his wife, who had contracted cancer when in her mid-thirties. His girls were quite unsettled when I met them, unsure of their own independence and really desperate for a mother, for their own had been taken from them in such a painful, desolating way.

I loved them immediately. We became great friends. For more than a year we went everywhere together, ate, sang, told jokes, played games together.

Audrey, the youngest one, was four. She was a beautiful child, with black hair and deep brown eyes, a charming and ready smile. But she was also quite willful. Her occasional tantrums were frightful to behold. But I found myself loving her deeply and identifying somewhat with her great loss. How I cherished those children.

Rachel, the older child by six years must have been very much like her mother as Sol described her to me. Sweet to a fault and thoughtful of others, Rachel was her mother's replacement in the family, making sure her father was happy, sharing school stories with him and later with me. She helped with cooking, cleaning and so many other things. She and Audrey had a great sibling rivalry going for the love of their father, but they made room in their hearts for me, and I am ever grateful for their understanding and care. I know that both these girls have grown up to become wonderful Jewish wives and mothers.

I thanked God I was so lucky. And eventually their father and I married in the temple with a *rabbi* officiating. Our reception was well attended. Everyone danced and told Jewish jokes. We were a family, happy and united. At last I could become a wife and mother. Every day I thanked God for my great blessings.

How many happy times we had! We attended Sabbath services together on Friday nights and Saturdays. My husband was kind and gentle. In accordance with Jewish tradition he cared for our needs and provided for us.

For a long time our marriage was blessed. We prayed together, celebrated the Jewish holidays with the girls, teaching them Jewish wisdom and customs. Their mother had been Jewish also. She taught them about their clothes and their outward appearances, their behavior in general. I tried to concentrate on inner development, urged them to develop kindness to one another. I stressed the meanings of the *shabbat* services and the propriety a young Jewish girl should have.

We joined dance schools and art classes. We went to mother-daughter luncheons at the synagogue. We took nature walks outside our home in one of the better parts of San Diego, making note of all the trees and shrubs, the habits of birds, the names of the neighbors. We talked about life, about God, about where their mother might be in Heaven and how she was looking down upon all of us and wishing us the best of all things.

In 1974 my brother married Mahlea, a Polynesian woman from Tonga. She was a Mormon, committed to her special way of life. She was related through a cousin to the king of Tonga. She had grown up there, beloved by everyone, part of their LDS community. She had come to Hawaii on a visit to a relative and there had met my brother, who by this time had moved up the California coast to the San Jose area. He had become an excellent bowler. In a contest he won a trip to Hawaii after bowling an almost perfect game. He and Mahlea met quite by accident. Their courtship was intense. They came back to the southwest and married soon afterward, deciding to find work together as a team in the restaurant business.

I did not meet Mahlea for a long time but I was immediately struck by her great dark beauty and her kind demeanor. She was truly a gentle soul, generous to a fault and loving of everyone. She deeply impressed me as the most beautiful spirit I had ever known. Finding out that she was a Mormon impressed me. I wondered what she knew that I did not, but we did not talk about religion very much at that time.

Eventually my brother converted to the LDS faith, saying he wanted eternal life in God's presence and had been assured he could receive it if he were worthy. I think his conversion changed my life, too. I was amazed he could leave Judaism behind, though he was not raised with a strong Jewish education. It is better, I thought, to be an atheist. I questioned him about it several times. He had experienced a conversion when faced with great personal difficulty. He had a new and strong witness that Jesus was the Christ and was challenged by his wife to join the Church. He wanted to be with Heavenly Father and Christ forever, he said, and as a Jew, without baptism into God's true church, that could never be possible.

"How do you know it's real?" I asked him. "How do you know Christ *is*?" Like most Jews I didn't know anything about death or resurrection. I have heard that there are increasing numbers of organizations which advocate Jews for Christ. This is a major step in the right direction.

More than his answers which followed the basic doctrinal assurances of the LDS church, I remember my brother's attitude. He had spent many years searching for happiness, also. He had to deal with the pain of a broken home, the search for happiness and a decent income to feed his wife and children. Now as I looked at him I saw peace in his face and a certainty I had never seen before. And then he said quietly:

"Christ is alive, sis. We can live with him and Heavenly Father forever in his kingdom if we accept him. I hope you'll investigate the Church some day. You could really use Christ in your life."

"I have God in my life," I threw back at him. "That's enough." But he only repeated himself softly. "Christ lives, too," was all he would say. I thought about that for a long time. My brother gave me a Book of Mormon and urged me to read it, which I did not do. It was a long history of early America. It had little effect on me at the time. Finally, I put it away, but I remember it felt unusually heavy in my hands. What I did browse through was done secretly because I was determined that my family should not think I was interested in some strange new religion. I thought my brother had made a mistake, and that eventually he would rectify it. Eventually I forgot about the book altogether.

Since my brother and I lived a thousand miles apart, I accepted his change and wished him well. He had found happiness in his own way and that was enough for me. I knew I could never accept a Christian way of life. Hadn't God chosen the Jews to be His people of the Abrahamic covenant? Wasn't worship of Christ as a Savior a violation of the first Commandment as expressed in Exodus 20:3? Since, in my mind the answers to both questions were affirmative, the only equation to the problem was that Christianity was in error. I really felt sorry my brother could be so easily misled...

# Chapter Two

People of the First Covenant


1.

*Out of the depths have I called Thee, O Lord.  Lord, hearken unto my voice; Let thine ears be attentive to the voice of my supplications.  Psalm 130  Masoretic text*

As the years passed my fortunes changed again.  Despite all of our efforts to make a happy life, my husband and I came to agree only upon divorce.  We both felt we had somehow made a mistake in marrying.  When I left our home I was sick at heart.  My grief was so great that I did as so many people do in their times of greatest need of help and consolation.  I decided not to seek God's help.  Attending services alone became no more than a lonely reminder that my family was not beside me.  Though we still loved each other, that love did not sustain us through the many problems we had to face.  Eventually togetherness became impossible.  I turned away from God when I most needed His help.  Still, I managed to attend some synagogue services, always feeling somewhat better afterward.

That time was really the start of my wanderings.  Without the Holy Spirit to guide me, without the knowledge of a loving Savior, I was truly lonely.  Even now it's difficult to recall the many times I ached for the children I missed so deeply and who depended upon me for a mother's love.  I missed the security we found in each other.

I knew I would always be a Jew, but for the most part now, an absentee from the synagogue.  There are times when people feel that the best advice is to listen to their own inner voice, moving with it as they are led by it, forgetting that their own reasoning is not a divine voice and can never be a safe guide to behavior.  Human reason is only what we have accumulated in knowledge about our morals and our choices.  Even with experience of life, reason alone is never enough to guide us.  We need divine help.

2.

*Shema Yisroel, adonai elohenu,adonai echad.*
*Hear O Israel, the Lord God, the Lord is One.*
*The Shema.  Jewish Creedal Prayer*

If I questioned the need of God in my life, I certainly did not think about it as Friday night services began with the *Shema*, the sacred creedal Jewish prayer that I loved. It is an affirmation of God's unity. The *Shema* statement refers to the ancient community of Israel which was made up primarily of Jews, the children of the state of Israel, and also the children of Israel of the Old Testament - the *Torah* - referring to the descendents of Jacob (see Gen 32:29). The Friday sunset service commemorates the beginning of Sabbath which lasts through sundown on Saturday. One reason for beginning a new day at sundown is given in Genesis 1:5, where it states that God created evenings before mornings. Each day, therefore, begins with the evening before it.

Saturday in the synagogue - the Jewish Sabbath day - the *Torah* is read. It is a time of great reverence, devotion, and sanctification. Sabbath services are a time when blessings are given by parents to their children. It is symbolic of the children of Israel who give praise to God for their eternal *Torah* (teachings), the Law of Moses. The *Torah* contains the Old Testament books of Genesis, Exodus, Leviticus, Numbers and Deuteronomy. The section on the Prophets is also included.

Before the morning Sabbath meal it is appropriate to recite the *Kiddush* (sanctification) prayer in Hebrew if possible, based upon Exodus 31:16-17 and Exodus 20:8-11, then to bless the meal, which Jews may do before and after eating. Wine and bread start the meal. They are symbols of the grape and grain God gives us to make a perfect balance in our lives. Sabbath afternoon includes *Torah* study, time spent with friends, sleep, perhaps a walk. In the afternoon there are additional services where the *Torah* is read in part. This is in remembrance of Jewish temples of old. The men go to the synagogue for services. This service is usually attended by the men only, but I attended with my father several times. Evening prayers often begin with the Hebrew words "*Vehu rahum*" (God is compassionate). Other ritual prayers are said before the final "*Shavua Tov*", when a good week is wished to all.

*You are One, your Name is One. Where else is there on earth a single tribe like Your People Israel, one and unique? Sabbath poem*

The Sabbath service stresses the idea of redemption of a people - the Jews have been indestructible. As a civilization they have survived time, denigration, attempts at annihilation, destruction and dispersion. Every Sabbath they give thanks for the miracle of endurance, a gift of God's compassion upon them.

On the Sabbath, Jews do not forget their animals, either. The fourth

Commandment, which ordains the Sabbath, tells us not to work even the cattle. The great *rabbi* and sage Maimonides tells us in the *Mishnah Torah*:

>*If one finds two animals, one burdened so heavily it is falling to its knees and the other animal is unburdened because the owner lacks help in loading it, it is his obligation to first unload the burdened animal.*
>*Laws of Murder and Preservation of Life, 13:13, Talmud*

On the Sabbath, Jews bless their children. Jewish parents are strongly obligated to teach their children about *Torah* and God at an early age. A common prayer is for the children to become like the greatest of Jewish heroes and matriarchs.

3.

*May God make you like Ephraim and Menashe.*
*May God make you like Sarah, Rebecca, Rachel and Leah.*

Why have we been saved? We are a *diaspora* (dispersed) people. Why, after all the afflictions, persecutions, wars and destruction of millions of Jews, does a Jew still delight in being part of the Abrahamic covenant which promised the seed of Abraham, Isaac and Jacob that they would multiply to fill the earth? Jews are taught through reading and revering *Torah* that they are a people chosen by God as special emissaries for several reasons. They have known God longer. They have accepted the Commandments and the hundreds of moral laws He offered them. They also agreed long ago to bear witness of Him in all they do. For an enlightening scripture, see Gen. 22:17.

*You are One, your Name is One. Where else is there on earth a single tribe like your people Israel, one and unique?*
*Union Prayer Book Sabbath recitation*

There were many ancient crises of faith in Judaism. The Old Testament records them. The Babylonian captivity of the Jewish people after the destruction of the First Temple and the razing of the Second Temple by the Romans were two such terrible times of crisis. Then the mass suicide at Masada, an ancient fortress where many Jewish zealots retreated from Roman captivity, dying by each other's hand to escape captivity and death when the Romans finally reached the Jewish fortress. In these instances and many more, Jews fought battles to retain their way of life. They were severely tested in their love of God in charity toward their opponents. That we are still here is testimony that we did not give in. The *Mishnah* says:

*In a war of self-defense, all go out to do battle, even a groom from his room, and the bride from under the wedding canopy.  Sotah 8:7*

4.

At that time in my life, however, the Jewish past did nothing to sustain me.  Despite the beauty of the Sabbath services and the hope, though subtle, that God is interested in my welfare, I felt no inner peace.  I realize now it was partially because I had little faith in God's blessings and no one else to care for.  Eventually I turned to a unique kind of service.

I returned to college in the winter of 1985, earning a Linguistic certificate which enabled me to teach English As a Second Language in schools and as a private tutor.  Because of the heavy influx of Ethiopian, Cuban and Vietnamese people into our cities during the early I980's, there was a tremendous need for teachers of English in the refugee centers.   I became a volunteer with the Catholic Resettlement Center, a branch of the Catholic diocese in San Diego.  There I was put to work teaching my language to hundreds of refugees in a classroom setting as well as on a one-to-one basis.

I don't know how to describe the beautiful spirits of the people I met during the three years which followed except to say their faith in God was unshakeable, as was their intense need for personal freedom as newly liberated individuals and as recent warriors of freedom in their war torn countries abroad.  They all had that in common.  I never saw animosity, disrespect or even lack of politeness among the crowds of various nationalities of refugees in that school.  They were newly born in America, fortunate inheritors of political freedom so passionately fought for by their countrymen a relatively short time before.  I was sympathetic to them.  We traded stories.  I told them of my Jewish ancestors, the European, *Ashkenazic* Jews who came to America during the first years of this century.

The *Ashkenazim* were German Jews originally from the Rhineland area about 300 B.C.E.  During the intervening century there were so many running from the purges, so many millions of European Jews finding new homes in western Europe, that now the term includes Polish and Russian Jews as well as the Jews of western Europe in general.  Our family is proudly *Ashkenazic.*

Many of these people I taught were illiterate in their own languages, which made it much more difficult to teach them English.  Because they lacked a discipline for language they had little sensitivity to its subtleties.  Many knew only one or two Americans at most and had no homes, no money or clothes.  The Catholic church got them started, welfare kept them going.  A sensitive teacher soon also became social worker and contributor. But it was great fun and so rewarding. They were so wonderful to work with. We loved each other. We became great friends.

I remember in particular Saddai, a lovely young woman and a war widow from Ethiopia, one of the small countries to the north of and bordering the Red Sea. Saddai told me that she, her eight year old son and her brother's teenaged son (who she passed off as her own to officials) literally walked out of Eritrea, their homeland, not long after the fighting over Eritrea's independence began. Of the more than three million Ethiopians living in an area about the size of Ohio, Saddai's family was among the thousands of peaceful Ethiopian people being murdered, raped and made to defend themselves and their homes during the horrible 1993 war for independence between Eritrea and Ethiopia. Annexed to Ethiopia by the British in 1962, the small state of Eritrea fought for its independence for more than thirty-one years.

Saddai was one of many widows who had lost their husbands in that war. Taking few provisions she fled with the two boys through the mountains, nearly perishing from cold and starvation on several occasions, relying on Eritrean sympathizers to offer them shelter for a few hours. They walked for a month until they found refuge in a church. Eventually the Catholic church included Saddai and the boys in their resettlement program. Through sponsors she and the boys were brought to San Diego where they were introduced suddenly into American culture. It was very difficult for them to adjust. They were displaced North Africans, alone except for each other in a fast-moving American city where they would have to endure racial prejudice, the welfare system and the shock of assimilation into a modern, English-speaking culture.

Many of the men and women whom I taught told me how they had fought the Ethiopian army in hand to hand combat. Entire families were often the victims. Finally, in their anger and grief thousands of them formed lines and during one night walked the many miles over the Ethiopian border into neutral Sudanese territory where they could find safety and eventual emigration to Italy, England and America.

I found many whose families had been broken apart, the older members as well as the children murdered. Many survivors of that long battle were severely disabled physically and mentally when they arrived in San Diego. With few exceptions they still firmly believed they would eventually return to Eritrea when independence was finally won. However, after being exposed to modern apartments, steady wages and benefits, most of the refugees I met decided to remain in America where they could save money to support relatives still in Eritrea while sending their children to large public and private schools. These refugees developed very mixed feelings about returning to a country devastated by war when the comforts of American life were becoming commonplace to them.

But there were still concerns about the safety of living in open societies. Many were perpetually afraid to give out their names because they feared the Communists in their own country would find them and try to have them deported Others feared the idea that we in America have some police who hate refugees, intent upon dragging them from their new shelters and depositing them once again in their besieged countries to die of famine or to be shot by their own countrymen for trying to escape certain torture and death.

All but the Cubans. They had no fear of deportation. They were the criminals who Castro had emptied out of his jails onto our shores. They couldn't go back. No one wanted them. They all came to stay here in America to partake of all we have to offer. They were like children, naughty but wonderful to teach.

I felt these people needed to know there were caring people in this country; that they were welcomed as part of the polyglot fabric of this society, as my own family had been only a generation before. In the years that passed I tutored many Ethiopian, Cuban and European men and women, assisting them with their social needs, explaining government restrictions, giving them driving lessons, purchasing groceries, counseling, teaching wherever possible. I attended their dances, ate their exotic foods, played with their babies and, as I could, shared their pain of exile from their own countries, in most cases causing permanent estrangement from their families.

I remember one day I asked my grandfather, my *Zaydeh*, about the Hebrew words *Gemilut Chesed* (loving kindness). "What should I learn from this?" I asked.

"It is greater than charity, my *madele*. Charity is done with money but *Gemilut Chesed* can be done by the person giving selflessly. Charity is given to the poor while loving kindness may be given to anyone. We can be charitable to the living but loving kindness can be lavished on the living and the dead alike."

Somewhere in those many heartfelt moments I learned something of great value. I saw the trust these refugees put in God and in Christ; how they went to church and praised both deities; how they lived careful, moral lives when they could have adopted our American ways and become carnal. I heard them pray in Tigrinian, in Polish, in Czechoslovak, in Spanish, in Vietnamese dialects, in Cuban. I heard their amazing stories of exodus, saw their grief as they read of the deaths in wars now far away on other continents. But always I saw their enduring faith in a Supreme Being and in Jesus Christ.

I think that is when I fully realized that God loves all his children and that I, too, must be a child of God. Was there something to the idea of Christ? A great many people seemed to pay him homage. In those crowds of refugees straining to learn English, praying feverishly for strength and for a place to begin again in this confusing, indifferent foreign land I often felt I was the only outsider.

Of the many things I learned in those years spent with the refugees, one primary idea became crystallized. That idea is simply that God transcends human thought. He is all knowing and all powerful. Even the awareness that there is a Heavenly Father, a divine power, is central to our identity as a race, for we are created in His image, by Him, to one day return to His presence.

We need this knowledge to accomplish anything of lasting value. *Torah* teaches us that we are responsible for our choices. A Jew believes he essentially has only the present, the now to live in. We must live worthy of being judged by God as righteous throughout our lives and hereafter.

5.

While we as Jews need not all behave in the same manner during our daily lives it is imperative that we follow the commandments given to us by *Torah*. The doing of good deeds can be more important in many instances than sharing identical creeds. Therefore, Judaism has several types of congregations (See Glossary). But all Jews share a central thematic set of truths:

A) There is one God who is the all knowing creator of the universe, eternal and indescribable. He is first and He is last. We must pray only to Him. Only ancient prophets are true ones. Like many Christians, the Jewish people do not think there is or can be new revelation, at least until their *Mashiach* comes to take them back to Israel, their promised homeland. They revere Moses, the most miraculous prophet of all, to whom God gave *Torah*. No new revelations, Jews believe, can be equal to *Torah's* teachings. God rewards good and punishes evil.

*There was an exchange of ideas between one Rabbi Kotzker and his disciples (pupils):*
*"Where does God exist?" the rabbi asked.*
*"Everywhere," the pupils answered, surprised.*
*"No, the rabbi replied. "He exists only where a man lets him in."*

B) In Jewish thought mortals cannot know God. His glory and greatness cannot be questioned, confined to a body, or even imagined. There is a Hebrew name for God but it is sacred to a Jew and should not be said without reverent respect. I was taught not to say it above a whisper lest it anger the Almighty. In Hebrew the sacred and mystical name for deity is written as *YHVH*. There are no vowels because the ancient Hebrew language has only consonant letters. Vowel sounds are added by diacritical marks. When pronounced with the diacritical marks the word takes on the sound of vowels, sounding something like *Yaweh*. To this day I do not say it, but I know there is a special and sacred name for my God which is all the more special because it is written in a holy tongue.

C) A Jew actively seeks the justice of God; to know how worthy he is in the sight of his Maker. Whenever he thinks he has the answers to all questions the Talmudic writings contain more questions. The search for knowledge and interpretation of scripture never falters, never ends, yet never reaches full understanding. Jews are supposed to question the teachings, to ask God to explain to them His mysteries.

D) The *Talmud*, another holy book of Judaism, seeks to interpret the *Torah* books. It contains the philosophies, the wisdom and the searching questions asked by *rabbis* from ancient times to the present century, as they contemplate and seek inspired interpretation of the Law of Moses for their congregations. (But can we know the Divine Mind if we do not admit to ongoing revelation?) Jews are bound by Mosaic law and must live within those boundaries, experiencing the present, revering their unique, often spectacular past. My hesitancy in accepting latter-day revelation about the nature of God, was due to my knowledge of *Torah*'s teachings about Him.

E) Jews believe God to be the creator of all space but too great to be confined within it. To a Jew, God has no body, though He is enduring and can take the shape of a man if He wishes. He doesn't dwell in a heaven or anywhere known to us, but has elevation above all. Time and space have no reference to Him, nor is He subject to change. He can be known through faith and good works. He is God of Israel. As we go to Him in personal prayer we can only hope He will be merciful to us but we are responsible for our own lives and destiny while we are alive. After death, we know He will not forsake us, but we know little of the world to come after our deaths. It isn't clearly stated in *Torah*. Much confusion and ignorance inevitably result unless one is willing to read the New Testament to see how Christ explained immortality.

6.

*Let not your heart be troubled: ye believe in God, believe also in me. In my Father's house are many mansions: if it were not so, I would have told you. I go*

*to prepare a place for you. And if I go and prepare a place for you, I will come again, and receive you to myself; that where I am, there ye may be also.*
*John 14:1-3*

While I was teacher to the refugees I began to significantly deviate from Jewish thought. Often I found myself asking the one question I had never allowed myself to consider relevant to my personal growth and happiness: Is Jesus the Messiah? How can so many people love him so fervently, as I love God, if Jesus was only a great teacher?

While I was teaching English to that small Eritrean community I often accompanied them to their Roman Orthodox Church. All their social events were solemnized there: the marriages, the baptisms, the family gatherings which met there to pray and to give thanks to their Savior Jesus Christ for bringing them to this new land of promise. The children were taught to worship. Pictures of Jesus were everywhere in their homes. Their food was blessed in Tigrinian (an Ethiopian language) and Italian, but I rarely saw anyone sit down to a meal without giving thanks for it to Jesus Christ. They knew I was a Jew but they seemed to want me to participate in these things with them. So that I wouldn't appear to be ungrateful when they prayed in this way, I also bowed my head.

New questions slowly became important to me: Are there advantages to believing in Jesus? Can I be a Jew and still believe Jesus is the Messiah? If Christ lives, should I accept him as my Lord? Is there one true church of Jesus Christ? Could it be, I wondered while I drove, while I tried to sleep, as I worked with students, while I ate, could it be that Jewish doctrine has omitted the acceptance of Jesus as the Savior in error? Such thoughts are blasphemy to a righteous Jew. Though I was not orthodox any longer I was ashamed to be thinking it.

But how could I reconcile all my differences? Impossible as that seemed, I found myself being led toward the answers.

# Chapter Three
Seek and Ye (also) Shall Find

1.

In those days I was always in need. I found employment as a hospital clerk. Living alone was difficult for me. I was young and interested in having a family of my own, but good opportunities never seemed to occur. Seeing the family strength of these refugees I yearned for a happy marriage and a permanent home of my own. But increasingly the refugees were becoming family, to each other and to myself. Their many plights were challenges for all to solve. Many times all I could do was to soothe them in their loneliness for lost or absent family members, their ancestral homes. Their grief became my own. How I prayed to God for their happiness.

I was not often attending *schul* during this time of my life. Reading the Old Testament I was reminded of the plight of the Hebrew refugees of Moses' time and that it is not unlike the refugees I was coming to know. Thousands of years ago people suffered but survived wars and forced migrations. Despite their hardships and pain of displacement they embraced God, asking for help and forgiveness from sin. I also petitioned God for these people but I felt no solace in synagogue, no reassurance from reading scripture. I was really dissatisfied with the Jewish congregations which seemed to me to be concerned only with their temporal needs and the Zionist movement. I felt caught between cultures: one preoccupied with an ancient past, the other a real and vital small foreign population struggling to survive in new surroundings and to make sense of what was happening to them.

2.

There was a Church Of Jesus Christ of Latter-day Saints near my home. One blustery day, feeling drawn there, I cautiously approached the front door of the chapel. Finding it open, I went in and gingerly sat down near the back, afraid to come nearer to the pulpit. The chapel around me was empty, the walls barren of pictures of Jesus Christ or symbolic crosses.

The entire chapel was made like a fortress: strong, well designed and constructed in a matter of fact way, as though business was conducted there and those many seats were often taken by people who came to get things done, to perform duties. It reminded me of a synagogue in its austerity, similar in its lack of symbolic detail except for the cabinet which housed the *Torah* scrolls behind the pulpit in the synagogue. The scrolls are always encased near the Eternal Light, which gives the Jewish people the assurance that their God is always with them. That sacred Light had always lit a candle of hope in my lonely heart.

Sitting in the silence I felt better but still uneasy because it was a church. Suddenly the door swung open and the janitor walked in. He was startled by my presence. "Are you waiting for someone?" he asked diplomatically. He was kindly but inquisitive, holding a rag in his hand. I guessed he'd heard the large front church doors open and had come to investigate. I was embarrassed and stood to leave. I had been found out. I half expected him to stare at me a minute and then say in amazement "Why, you're a Jew, aren't you?" and immediately phone a *rabbi* to come get me!

"I'm sorry. I came only to pray," I apologized. " If the church is closed, I'll leave," I said, almost relieved to be discovered. The janitor's face softened. "Oh, no. If you came here to pray, then you stay. You must need to be here or you wouldn't have come on a rainy day," he laughed. Turning, he softly closed the door behind him. I sat down again, thankful but unsure as to why, and began attending to business with real purpose.

I prayed to God to help me with so many things: my car, my job, my loneliness, my desire to be happy. Somehow, I felt I was not alone. I kept looking behind me, for it seemed someone was there, but I saw no one. It was a long time before I left the chapel and when I walked to my car I had the feeling, for the first time in my life, that some Presence had heard me. I knew that I had not been alone in that chapel. It was unnerving, but I felt warm and good and cried on the way home.

That was just the beginning. The next day I found a good mechanic to fix my car. My employer told me I was doing well. Relatives called from out of town. I had a great day! It stopped me dead in my tracks. Did something-- someone -- hear me? Were my prayers heard? I was amazed to think personal prayers could actually be answered specifically and quickly. The next week I returned to the chapel. After a while it became an irregular but a certain routine. Every time I went to church and prayed for understanding and help, it came. Within a day or two I found help or the need for help dissipated and I found the strength to deal with my problems. I began to think "I have to get to church and tell God what I need now."

I never told anyone about the phenomenon that I had discovered. It was like a well of wondrous healing power that seemed inexhaustible and which I, a Jewish woman, was receiving freely just for praying earnestly. After a while I stopped worrying about it, walked boldly into that chapel, said hello to the janitor, sat down and talked openly to God. It felt great. Those hours will always be among the most cherished of my life. It was, of course, the beginning of my testimony of Heavenly Father. The Lord was leading me to His truth.

What had I discovered? How many hours did I spend contemplating that answer? Who is the "Lord," I wondered. Is Jesus the Messiah? Is he *Yeshua*? I searched the Psalms for wisdom I had learned in Hebrew school years ago. I came to this advice in Psalm 55:22: "*Cast thy burden upon the Lord and He will sustain thee.*" But I was still afraid to realize the importance of my discovery because if these experiences were real, there was only one answer. I still knew little about Jesus and nothing of the Mormon church, but I did realize one great truth, and to this day I have never had reason to question it: I had found a place where I knew God visited on this earth. At last I knew where to find Him. He was waiting for me when I entered The Church of Jesus Christ of Latter-day Saints.

It will be difficult for a Mormon to understand, but for a Jew who has been educated in Judaic law to enter a "church" of any other faith and to find solace there is heresy. Who can know the mysteries of God or where He is and is not, for is He not everywhere? But not to find peace in the synagogue was one of the hardest mysteries to reconcile. I was afraid to look within a church for answers, afraid of the New Testament, The Book of Mormon and any other Christian literature which might, after all, lead me to the understanding my heart really wanted but that my family and my religious upbringing forbade.

3.

I have run away to *schul* this night. It is the last evening of *Sukkot*, the Jewish harvest festival which is celebrated for seven days every September. Work is forbidden on the eighth day because it is a feast day (See Lev. 23:34-56). I have joined the congregation to be among them in their joy and to hear once again the reading of the *Simchat Torah* (a portion of scripture). This night the yearly cycle of *Torah* readings is completed and begun again for the following year. Reading the *Torah* helps Jews to link this event to their heritage in Egypt (See Deut 16:13-15). On this holiday we offer our substance to God. We are His co-workers. We dedicate our lives and our work to him.

I watch with happiness and anticipation as the *Torah* scrolls are taken from the ark which holds them. The *rabbi* leads the procession around the congregation. We stand and sing and clap for joy. We sing in celebration of the holy scriptures but while I celebrate the joy... I feel the pain of separation. I recall my maternal grandmother's stories of how the families in her small village were denied a Jewish education and the right to celebrate holidays by the brutal Russian government. How glad she was to come to America. "Now Jews can dance the dance of life - *am Yisroel hay!*"

4.

At first I would not accept that step as a signally important life move. Such things are rarely recognized in the bud. In fact, I promptly began living a double life. Friday nights I travelled across town to attend Sabbath services, feeling out of sorts with it but knowing it to be my duty as a Jew. I loved the *cantor*'s songs of prayer complementing the *rabbi's* sermons. The *cantor* or singer sets the tone of Hebrew prayer as he sings in mournful intensity before the congregation. I loved to see the *Torah* brought forth on the Jewish holidays. With all my heart I gave thanks to God for that wondrous scriptural set of moral laws and for my own life, for my kindred Jews and for our unique faith.

As part of my double life, in the anonymity of daytime I would surreptitiously drive to the newly discovered LDS chapel to pray again in greater earnest. I even visited LDS chapels across town just to see if I felt the same entity listening to me in every one of them. Truly, I always knew I was heard. I was amazed.

When I went to Heavenly Father with only the smallest faith but with a real need, with contrition, asking to be heard, I received many answers, though I was not aware of His promises or of His love for me until much later. How strange it seemed that by going outside my religion I had taken an important step in increasing my faith and hope for a better life.

I don't mean to imply that God does not dwell among the Jews in their synagogues or among any people or church who are righteous and who ask for His help. His forgiveness and love are bestowed in abundance and willingly given to those who love Him. I only mean that I could not find the assurance and serenity or the feeling of a Presence in the synagogues I attended to compare with the feelings and promptings I received in the LDS chapel, and much later in the LDS temples. I came to know later on that the Holy Ghost - a personage of spirit and a member of the Godhead which includes God and His Christ - only sanctifies edifices which have been dedicated by those having proper priesthood authority through the Melchizedek priesthood as it has been restored to the earth in these latter days. (See citations in The Book of Mormon as well as Doctrine and Covenants Sections 20, 84, 112, 121, others)

In my search for personal faith and reassurance I wanted to experience a spiritual feeling that I was loved, listened to and taken seriously by my Creator. During my lifetime I have sat in many types of churches with many friends of many persuasions and felt only mild interest. I wasn't ready then to receive the promptings of the Holy Ghost who testifies to us that God lives and that Jesus is the Christ. But I had evinced a divine outpouring for the first time that day in the LDS church. I was being strongly prompted to search further.

A Jew who pursues the path of discovery which I was beginning to follow - one that leads to belief in Christ, his apostles and an organized church bearing his name - risks the great anger of friends and family. Therefore, when I experienced religion as a Christian does, through the agency of Christ, I was unsure about investigating the phenomenon. My earlier knowledge of Christianity came almost exclusively from some of poet John Milton's work in "Paradise Lost" and other works on the divinity of God and the Devil's influences. Maybe I thought I could change boats without rocking either one. I had growing curiosity then, but not much courage.

*5.*

*When I first saw him in my dreams he was standing among the books of Hebrew, chanting a soft prayer. My maternal grandfather, my Zaydeh, Israel Simkovitz. How fervently he had wanted to become a rabbi to lead his congregation as a man of God in his hometown near Minsk. How dearly he loved the Torah and the commentaries. He often quoted the teachings of the great Rabbi Moses Maimonides. He arose early each day to give the birkhots (daily prayer honoring God's holiness) with his family. How devoted he was. I revered him. Seeing him now, I moved toward him.*

*"Zaydeh! How good to see you." He hugged me, then held me at arm's length and looked at me for a long minute. His eyes began to fill with tears. "Maydele (little girl), why do you come to me as a Jew when your heart longs for another god?"*

*I shrank back in shock. How could he know what I dared not admit to myself? "I am a Jew, Zaydeh. Nothing has changed."*

*"Yes, it is changing," he insisted. "You are looking for the Mashiach and he has not come. Hallow the name of Jehovah, our one God. Make yourself in His image alone. You, a part of my flesh, you are a Jew. A Jew! A Jew cannot believe in Christ!"*

*His face hardened and then softened in sadness. It was as though I had already found some Christian church and told him I was converting.*

*Oh, how my heart ached. My soul was filled with anguish. How I wanted to please him, to read Torah with him, to feel secure that my Jewish education was all I would ever need. But there was more to discover.*

*"Zaydeh, maybe there is something to the idea of Jesus being the Savior. Many people have built churches to him. Are they all wrong? Where is the Mashiach? How do you know for sure he has not already come to us?"*

*He thrust out a book of scripture at me. "Here, read the Torah. Moses had no Jesus. Isaiah had no Jesus. Worship God! You are a Jew!" He turned and walked away from me, disgusted, through the room of books. I stood there, knowing somehow that a line had been crossed, that I could never again be young and accepting. Somewhere in my heart of hearts, with great guilt, I had secretly begun the search for my Redeemer.*

6.

My brother somehow knew what I needed. From his church ward in Oregon he requested that LDS missionaries in San Diego visit me, which they eventually did. During two of the most memorable months of my life I received lessons and visited the beautiful Mormon Battalion church in San Diego several times (always after services were over and everyone else had gone, because I refused to sit with the congregation. They were Christians, and I was a Jew. I felt we should remain separate).

Those missionaries were beautiful spirits. They patiently answered my questions, instructed me in the ways of the church, prayed for me and gave me unlimited access to church literature. They told me that God has a perfected body and that Jesus Christ really is God's only Begotten Son, born on earth as the child of a virgin through the influence of something they called the Holy Ghost.

They told me also that I had always lived and had chosen my path on this earth. I was very surprised to learn that I was going to be judged on all that I do and say and that there are differing degrees of glory in heaven following death. I had heard something of this through the mystical book called the *Kabbalah*, which is also a part of Judaism. But that work was essentially arcane conjecture.

By this time I had stopped attending the synagogue in order to allow myself what I believed was an unbiased period of time in which to absorb and to accept or reject the missionary teachings. My heritage, the memories of my upbringing, the songs of the *cantor*, all these were still strong in my mind and heart. I often resented the elders because the things they were teaching me were ideas I found myself wanting to believe, but I knew how it would change my life if I came to know these things were true. So whenever they asked me to pray about it, I didn't do it. Paradoxically, though I longed for the change I knew was necessary to my growth, I feared it almost as much!

But I found that whenever I let them take me to church and I touched the doors that I broke into tears. I was shocked and amazed, not understanding why, but the missionaries knew. They said it was the Holy Ghost testifying to me of the truthfulness of this Church.

For many of those precious moments they were all sure I was only a moment away from baptism and eternal happiness. Until they asked me for a commitment.

I knew that if I remained just outside any kind of commitment I would not anger my relatives (even though none of them lived near me I felt they were somehow aware of what I was thinking.) I did not want to make this crucial decision, even though I was learning quite a bit from the elders. I would not make that commitment. I remember my own great sadness that this wonderful episode of teaching was going to come to an end. I would not then accept that Joseph Smith was a true prophet of God. Nor could I be sure that The Book of Mormon is the word of God, though I had begun to read it. I was still unable to accept the idea or the reality of the Holy Ghost as a part of God's sacred influence, partly because I feared God and His judgement upon me if I were to take these new things lightly.

7.

*Whoever saves one life, it is as if he saved the entire world.*
*Mishna Sanhedrin 4:5. Quoted in Jewish Wisdom*

Several years passed. After graduating from the university I was attending I moved to Oregon to join my brother and his family. His wife had contracted cancer and was quite sick. They had four little ones to care for. Almost immediately I met a number of LDS members. We became friends. I also attended the small synagogue in my town, once again resuming my duty as a diligent Jewish woman, attending Sabbath services weekly while continuing a special, almost secret flirtation with the LDS church, living more and more within that rarified atmosphere, attending a few church functions now, (never any baptisms), cautiously, but always wondering, always questioning.

The process of change was so gradual. Once more I met the missionaries, and once more rejected them. I remember the day I made my decision. I had decided not to pursue the teachings, but I didn't know how to tell them nicely.  Angry because I did not want to make such a life-changing decision, I went to the church that Sunday and called the elders into the hallway where I told them not to come around any more.  I was going to remain a good Jew and stop flirting with Christian nonsense.  I remember the looks on their faces.  Instantly I felt sorry, but I had made my choice.  I drove home in a black mood of depression that lasted most of the week.  I didn't understand that, either, but at last it went away.  Now I was not in any danger of joining a church.

8.

A few months passed.  Through my brother and his sweet Tongan wife who loved the church I was growing close to a couple who were stake missionaries.  I will call them Betty and Dan.  Dan knew little of Judaism but he understood my hesitancy.  He told me something so simple it made an important impression upon me.

"Becoming a Mormon doesn't mean you cannot be a Jew or practice Jewish rituals.  It does involve adding onto what you already are.  You are going farther, adding upon what you already understand, accepting more knowledge."

His words helped.  I was still wrestling with the problem of accepting the principles of the Gospel as truth.  How could I remain a Jew and accept the Gospel of Christ?  Wouldn't I lose my identity as a Jew?  That is a serious consideration.  To agree that The Book of Mormon is true, that Joseph Smith received the keys to this final period of testing and winnowing of souls before the Millennium when Christ shall return, to be baptized and accept the companionship of the Holy Ghost - these things still seemed like heresy, far from *Torah* teachings, which hearkened back to the fifth century b.c.e.

I didn't know then how to ask for help through the power of Christ.  The sacrament procedure seemed a primitive ritual.  Its symbolism was alien to me and I was uncomfortable with it.  I felt that The Book of Mormon could never replace the importance and majesty which the *Torah*'s presence brought to my mind and heart when the scrolls are brought near the congregation during High Holy Day services.  The LDS chapel had no *Torah* scrolls, no Eternal Light and no Jews.  How could I listen to the Christian hymns so different from the Hebrew songs?  I never knew how captive I was to my faith until I found myself attracted strongly to another.

What if I abandoned my religion for one which wasn't the same as that steady old ship of Judaic antiquity, still afloat after several thousand years?  What would my God do to me?  I prayed even harder to be kept from making a mistake.

I could imagine my beloved seventy-year old Aunt Rose glaring at me, shaking her head, letting loose a heavy wail of grief if I should tell her about my interest in any church.  No, it didn't seem right to accept what could be in error just to get to join the LDS church and have my prayers heard and answered. Maybe I would just moonlight there for the rest of my indecisive life!

Feeling very drawn to Betty and Dan and wanting so much to solve my questions  once and for all, I made them a deal.  I offered to finance and help them build a room in the barn on their property and to move into that room.  It would not have running water, sink or bathroom, but would have electricity.  The main house was about twenty-five feet away.  In that room I would withdraw to study my religious books, their religious books, praying and studying until my prayers were finally answered and I knew once and for all the truth.  I vowed not to move out of that room until I knew the truth for sure.

Happily, they agreed.  Within a month the room was built and I moved into it.  I was forty.  I had no husband, no children, a part-time job I didn't like, not much money, lots of religious passion, but I was unable to decide what to believe.  What did I have to lose?

I began to read these new scriptures, The Book of Mormon, The Doctrine and Covenants, The Pearl of Great Price, with greater intensity than I had ever given any task.  To my great surprise it seemed that all the knowledge I had ever gained from the Old Testament was being carried forward, expanded, systematized and given much greater coherence in these other books.  I read for hours at a time, barely conscious of the passing of the hours or the hunger for food.  There was nothing to distract me and I read with more concentration and intensity than I had ever given to any task.  I began to understand how God works among us, leading us forward while He is far ahead, readying the next problem we will have to solve before moving on again.  I prayed often and in real earnest to know if these books were true. I waited for the confirmation Betty told me would most assuredly come.

9.

I remember clearly the first prompting I received.  It was a cloudy day in February.  I was driving my trusty old Toyota truck on some errand, momentarily stopped at a traffic light, waiting to turn a corner.  I was very weary, having spent a week in my room reading and praying and this outing was a treat I had given myself to get out for awhile.  As I sat looking at the red stoplight a thought went through my mind.

"Jesus Christ is the Messiah of the world." That was all. I sat at attention, in shock, staring at the stoplight. Could I have heard it right? Then, as quickly, the same sentence went through my head again. By this time the light had changed but there were no cars behind me so I just sat there thinking.

Suddenly, unemotionally, it seemed to make sense. People have been worshipping Christ for centuries. If he was the Messiah that the Jews have rejected, it would make sense that so many Christians abounded. If he was not the Annointed One he would have been forgotten!

I made an unplanned right turn, drove back to Betty's house and told her what had happened. She was very happy but not surprised. "You are being taught by the angels," she said. "The Lord wants you to come to him in his church and he is readying you."

I remember walking out, shaking my head in amazement, greatly surprised at this first revelation I had ever received. I vowed to study harder, longer, and with even greater intensity. The answers were beginning to come. Was I able to accept them? What good would all my study and prayer do if I received truth and was afraid to believe it? I vowed to let God lead me and teach me. I prayed eagerly now for the truth to be given me, for greater understanding of God's kingdom on earth, and the courage to accept the revelations that came to me. I finally felt I was making real progress!

Not long afterward, following much more reading, study and prayer, the assurance finally came. I love to tell how it happened.

Betty was in the hospital briefly and I was to bring her home. I arose that morning and dressed quickly. It was a cold day but not yet raining. If I hurried I would not keep her waiting. There was no time for breakfast. I walked outside and stood there buttoning my coat, noticing that I was alone. Dan was the only man who lived there and he was at work. Their kids were at school.

Suddenly, in the silence I clearly heard a voice, a man's voice, to my left, just above my ear. Turning, I saw no body. But I felt he was there. I felt his shape and height with my "spiritual" eyes.

The Presence spoke to me as one speaks with another. He told me I was free to make any choice I desired. Free. Not bound by any religion or any expectation. I was precious to the Lord and he had faith in me to make the right decision based upon the revelation of truth that was being given me. That was all, but after hearing his message I started to feel a tremendous pressure within myself, as if I was about to grow a second heart and my chest had to expand to make room for it.

This was the revelation I had prayed so diligently to receive! The words entered my heart and became like my own. I *was* free! My head was filling with singing, with new emotions, with new sensations. I felt what I can only describe as joy, the first time this emotion had ever come to me. And then I realized that this Presence had given me the one element I had been lacking in my attempt to accept or to reject forever the Gospel of Christ: I needed heavenly permission! I was waiting for a divine push!

I heard myself shout "If that is true, then I want to become a Mormon!"

And as I stood there looking upward, alone again, trying to understand what I had just felt, I realized that in that special, shining moment I had been touched by a force and power I had never known. All my doubts vanished. I *knew* the Gospel of Jesus Christ is true and perfect. The Church of Jesus Christ of Latter-day Saints *is* the restored true church of Christ upon the face of the earth today. Joseph Smith was and is a prophet of God and there is a living prophet on the earth today, just as I was taught by the missionaries. I was shaking with joy! The Articles of Faith are true. *Christ lives! He is the Messiah*, not of the Jews but of the world, and there most certainly is a Holy Spirit of God which communicates with mankind and who testifies of all truth!

The darkness of the past was swept away. My body filled with the light of discovery, from my feet to my head. I actually *vibrated* with a new energy. I had received a revelation which came from the Holy Ghost, and in that moment I knew the truth forever!

The certainty of it overwhelmed me and gave me wondrous feelings of happiness such as I have never known. Inside of an instant of time I knew my new mission was to become part of this divinely instituted church. I had taken *the leap of faith* and was rewarded with divine assistance.

I was also given the knowledge that I was not alone and that I would never be alone again, in a spiritual sense. That is the Plan of a loving God who made us all individually, created in His image, and who watches over each of us. A true convert to Jesus Christ is a new person, changed forever in spirit and body. I was on that day born again in Christ, no longer mine but his forever.

*Therefore, the redeemed of the Lord shall return, and come with singing unto Zion, and everlasting joy and holiness shall be upon their heads; and they shall obtain gladness and joy; sorrow and mourning shall flee away.*
*2NE 8: 11 (Book of Mormon)*

*"There is no fear in love; but perfect love casteth out fear..." 1John 4:18*

# Chapter Four

## The Mystery Unfolds

### 1.

In the weeks that followed my decision to become a Jewish convert to the Church, I felt the Spirit working on me, softening me, filling my mind with a gentleness I had never known. I recalled parts of scripture I had read years ago making sense to me. Suddenly I found myself quoting The Book of Mormon all the time, crying at work, crying in my room whenever I read the scriptures. Dan told me the tears indicated that the Holy Ghost was testifying to me of the truths I was learning. My hours were gradually filled with a new peace and understanding.

Most of all I developed a great thirst for knowledge about the religion, the scriptures, the beginnings of it all, and most importantly, about the life and times of Jesus. Though I had received revelation that The Church of Jesus Christ of Latter-day Saints is the restored church of Jesus Christ, I still needed to investigate the scriptures again to see how the Plan has been unfolded to us. Without also having a full understanding of church structure I could not understand what the apostle Paul told the Corinthians:

*"For as the body is one, and hath many members, and all the members of that one body, being many, are one body:  so also is Christ... "And the eye cannot say unto the hand, I have no need of thee... but God hath tempered the body together...that there should be no schism in the body;..." (See 1 Cor 12:12,21,25).*

### 2.

I wanted to know all about the Messiah and the government of Heaven. Most amazing of all, I no longer had doubts as to the authenticity of Mormon doctrine. It's almost as though I had for years really wanted to believe but wouldn't let myself accept it without divine permission. I had read it, loved it and finally was advised of its truthfulness, then urged to accept it by a power greater than any on earth. Now I needed to read again closely for a full understanding to gain a knowledge and a testimony. This would become a lifelong pursuit.

One question I always had as a Jew was about the uncertainty of life after death. What happens to the body and the spirit? Are they separated forever? Does the spirit lose life also after death comes to the body? The *Torah* does not deal with it and the *Talmud* can only speculate upon it, but in the New Testament the basic question is answered that Christ came to give us that eternal gift of the Resurrection. Only in Mormon doctrine, however, is there clarity given regarding the three kingdoms, what constitutes our worthiness to enter them (See Doctrine & Covenants 76), and where the spirit travels after death. I remember my tears as I read in Doctrines & Covenants 131:7:

*"All spirit is matter..."* which we all shall one day discover. In Alma 40:11 I read that when our spirits leave our bodies, they are *"...taken home to that God who gave them life."*

Another searing question I had was that of life before this one. Jews know they were somehow with God before birth, but have no firm understanding in that regard. How are we with God before our birth into this world? Do we have any say about our lives on this earth? Is reincarnation a true principle?

Answers were not hard to find when I really began searching for them in latter day scripture. I read about the Council in Heaven that I attended with all other spirits, where we chose our Savior, banished Satan, and chose to come here (See Alma 13:3, Doctrine & Covenants 29:30-37, Abr 3:22-26 Pearl of Great Price). We were valiant spirits in our pre-earth home. We were fervent in our desire to unite our spirits with bodies, to have children, to serve the Lord and prepare the way for his coming, to have joy as humankind.

Now I understand that the path I have chosen was foreordained. As I prayed in wonder to know the truth of these things I was assured that I had found the correct knowledge.

The Book of Mormon answered some very important questions for me. One was the question of Adam and Eve's transgression in the Garden. It has fascinated me with its intrigue. Just how guilty were they of disobedience? If God knew they would transgress, why did He allow it? Is it possible for man to be saved without repentance? (2NE 2:11-27, Moses 5:1-11)

The answers to these questions took more time and effort, but I discovered in Alma 12:24-30 and Alma 42 that Heavenly Father has given us this life that we might have time to use our free agency and to repent as necessary before our mortal lives are finished. I discovered that Adam did not unknowingly transgress, but was heroic because he chose to keep God's more important commandment, to multiply and replenish the earth. He therefore partook and followed his wife into mortal life.

If Adam and Eve had not repented of their choice to disobey God's first commandment to not eat of the tree of the knowledge of good and evil they *"...would not have accepted God's plan of redemption. With hardened hearts they could not have received God's mercy or entered into His rest."* *Alma 12:32-36)*

My understanding now is that if these first parents of ours had not with great courage and love for their unborn generations undergone their great transformation made possible by partaking of the forbidden fruit, I would not be here to read about it!

Another important question The Book of Mormon answered for me concerns the restoration of the Jews to their homeland of Israel. The Book of Mormon is written *"...to Jew and Gentile-."* To illustrate this point, there are 433 verses of Isaiah quoted in The Book of Mormon, many of which point to the mission of Jesus Christ among the Jews. I read with fascination 2Ne 15 as Isaiah tells that the transgressions of Israel (God's vineyard) will lead to their being scattered across the earth in *diaspora*. As a result of spiritual blindness and their refusal to live the Law of Moses and to recognize and accept Jesus Christ as their Messiah, the Jewish civilization brought down upon its head the wrath of God Who saw fit to cleanse them in sorrow and affliction:

*"Therefore, my people are gone into captivity because they have no knowledge; and their honorable men are famished, and their multitude dried up with thirst."* *2Ne 15:13. (See also Hosea 4:6)*

Because the Jews did not hearken unto Moses and their other great prophets they were cast out, thereafter to be subject to untold number of sorrows and miseries.

But The Book of Mormon tells us that redemption will come *"When the Lord shall have washed away the filth of the daughters of Zion, and shall have purged the blood of Jerusalem from the midst thereof by the spirit of judgment and by the spirit of burning."* *2Ne14:4*

The Lord will never forget his people and he will, in these latter days *"...lift up an ensign to the nations from far, and will hiss unto them from the end of the earth and behold, they shall come with speed swiftly; none shall be weary nor stumble among them."* *2Ne 15:26*

The knowledge of these truths gave me great assurance that what I was learning was indeed correct. And that certainty has never left me. My faith has become unwavering in its intensity and beautiful in its sustaining ability.  Most of all I had to realize I wanted to be committed to a spiritual way of life.  My hesitancy was due to my respect for heavenly affairs: I dared not be a religious hypocrite.  Because I am a Jewess, I had to honor those traditions.  The fight was between secular tradition and the restored truth.

3.

*For God so loved the world, that he gave his only Begotten Son, that whosoever believeth in him should not perish, but have everlasting life.  John 3:16*

I love this scripture.  It has become part of the basis of my new life.  My baptism on April 6, 1988 was joyous.  Dan baptized me and later said there were many spirits in the room with us.  I agreed I had also felt them there.  We were all so happy when the moment of truth came there in the water, for I knew there was no turning back, so I didn't hesitate.  I would have been declared dead by my family if they had been living then.  My aunt and uncle eventually did disown me when they found out that I had met some Mormon people.  That hurt, but it is a small price to pay.  My father had died several years ago, my mother had disappeared when I was much younger and my only sibling was already a member!  There was no immediate family to please anymore.

But I also knew my allegiance belonged to my Father in Heaven and to Jesus Christ, the *Mashiach*, for all time.  With the laying on of hands to receive the gift of the Holy Ghost, I was certain I had made the most important decision of my life and that it was the correct one.  To have only learned the truth but not to be baptized a member of Christ's restored church would have afforded me little.  The first two principles of the Gospel are faith and repentance.  Without actually allowing myself to be cleansed from sin and renewed in the water, then to receive the clarifying gift of the Holy Ghost, I could never be spiritually reborn, ready and inspired to follow my Master wherever he would lead me.  Now I could more fully understand the truth of the scripture which Paul so diligently wrote those new converts to the original church:

*Therefore, if any man be in Christ, he is a new creature: old things are passed away; behold, all things are become new.  2Cor 5:17*

4.

How can I describe my feelings on that blessed day?  For almost a half century I had identified myself as a Jewish woman, connected by my upbringing to a special past that stretched back to Canaan and forward to Judah.  All my life I had read books on Judaism, studied Hebrew tradition and read from the *Union*

*Prayer Book* (Jewish).   The rituals and traditions I had lived with were so removed from modern society that I had never even celebrated Christmas or sung a Christmas carol.   When it seemed that all the world carried Christmas toys into their living rooms in December and exchanged gifts on Christmas morning, my family turned away.   We turned up our noses and waited for the Festival of Lights, the eight day Jewish celebration known as *Hanukkah*.

Now I was baptized, a member of Christ's church.   A Christian!   A Jewish Christian!   A new person - one of a kind.   Every Jew who has joined the Church must have felt like I did that day and for a long time afterward.   An ocean had been crossed, a wall scaled.   There was no turning back.

But this day was filled with the peace and joy of the Spirit of God.   As I went through those first days after baptism I felt very different.   It took a while to understand that difference.   I was clean of sin.   Forgiven of all my trespasses.   They were forgiven and forgotten by God.

This new feeling of lightness brought me great relief.   My new friends said I was "golden."   I felt like a new person.   As the day of baptism wore on, a sweet and gentle feeling came over me.   I noticed a profound change beginning within me.   It made me very quiet.   Betty noticed it eventually.

"You're glowing," she said.   "Want to tell me what you're feeling?"

Her words struck me.   I was feeling new things, subtle yet very important to me.   I walked over to the mirror and gazed into it.   A white dress seemed to come into form around me and a softer image gazed back from the mirror.   My deepest wishes had been fulfilled.

"I feel like a bride of Christ," I replied to the image in the mirror.

5.

Why was my baptism the beginning of a new life?   The Jewish creedal statement, the *Shema*, is our first clue.   Even Christ reminded his followers: *Hear, O Israel, the Lord our God, the Lord is One (Mark 12:29)*.   He spoke of a unity of purpose, a oneness between mankind and our divine Maker because we are literally the spirit children of our Heavenly Father (See Moroni 7:22,24,28).

Baptism was an ancient Jewish practice used when Jews had sinned.   A ritual bath to cleanse of menstrual blood or sin was given.   In Orthodox Jewry this practice is sometimes still followed, called a *mikveh*.   But baptism among early Jews did not have the meaning or eternal consequences that Jesus brought to it.

I found part of my answer in the book of my second favorite prophet, Isaiah 1:16-18:

*Wash you, make you clean: put away the evil of your doings from before mine eyes; cease to do evil; Learn to do well; seek judgment, relieve the oppressed, judge the fatherless, plead for the widow. Come now, and let us reason together, sayeth the Lord: though your sins be as scarlet, they shall be as white as snow; though they be red like crimson, they shall be as wool.*

I thirsted for salvation. I hungered for forgiveness of past sins. Among my deepest and to that point unrealized desires was the desire to come forth as a child again; to begin life anew with the knowledge I had gained, to have another chance; this time with sanction and with help from my God who I had rediscovered so recently to be someone I could understand and get to know on a personal basis.

I wanted a clean slate, to be at peace, complete. Being baptized by the correct authority gave me that essential promise: If I kept my covenants as they were explained to me, I would always have the Holy Ghost to be my companion, to lead me through the trials in my life and to prepare me to return to the celestial kingdom. How I longed for that promise! How grateful I am to have finally become a member of God's church!

The following day I stood in Betty's kitchen making a small lunch. I kept hearing music in the room from a radio playing softly somewhere above me, though I did not recall seeing a radio in the kitchen. The music was sweet A choir was singing. How beautiful it was. I mentioned it to Dan.

"What station is playing on your radio?"
Dan listened a moment. "I don't hear anything," he said. "There's no radio in that room."

I listened again but this time the music had stopped. "Maybe it's the angels," he laughed. "They're glad you finally joined the Church."

Since that perfect hour of baptism and the reception of the gift of the Holy Ghost I have happily and diligently studied gospel doctrine to gain greater understanding of both Judaism and of Christianity. Though my own family is scattered, I want always to retain my heritage as a Russian Jewess and my blessings as a member of the ancient family of Judah.

At the same time I keep an eye open to an eternal perspective, intent upon my own salvation, mindful of my growth as a soul which needs daily spiritual nourishing, blessed with a mind which craves the wisdom of the eternities.

# Chapter Five

People of the New Covenant

1.

Religion is mysterious. I know that when I first heard of God I looked around to find a person and was told God was invisible, ever present, yet unknowable. I thought for a long time that it was impossible for a power to exist which could not be sensed directly or known to the ordinary mind. I thought that all those adults who believed in what they could never prove were crazy at best, having made it all up because they felt the need. I was the original cynic, raised with a whip and a cruel hand, at times certain the world could never boast a living God; usually certain there was no joy anywhere.

For much of my life before I was led to the church, I thought a lot about spiritual things. I wanted to know how everything began. In the human mind there is always the hunger to know the Infinite Mind, to imagine where humanity is in the universes and what forces have brought us here to suffer, to have joy, to long for an all encompassing Being who is comprehensible. How can we conceive of the Infinite? How can we hope for a final destination beyond the stars when we see no Deliverer? What is the vehicle that will get us safely back to heaven for eternity? It was the answers to these basic questions I was really seeking.

As I came to know various sisters in an auxiliary in the church called the Relief Society I heard many wonderful stories of baptisms, strong testimonies, promptings and revelatory dreams that many members have received. They really helped to strengthen my testimony of the Gospel. Over and over I realized I had done the right thing.

Shortly after I joined the church I met Esther, another Jewish convert, a woman in her 50's, happy and robust and with a great testimony of the restored Gospel. We became friendly and she told me this marvelous story about her husband, who had recently died.

Herschel was not a young man. He was about fifty years old, studying at a rabbinical college to become a *rabbi*. A devout Jew of European parentage, he had been studying *Torah* for years. At the end of his first year of rabbinical college he had a dream in which he saw an angel with his hand raised before him. The angel uttered one word: "Wait." Herschel, not knowing what to make of this dream, soon forgot it. He was not normally a dreamer. Toward the end of the second year he had the same dream and was very disturbed about it, but failing to understand it, he put it aside. During the next several years he dreamed of the angel again, always the same dream, always troubling. No one he talked to at the rabbinical college could advise him about it.

Finally the time came for Herschel to take final exams. Again he had the dream. This time the angel spoke to him more firmly, saying the same word, "Wait." Herschel felt the angel was telling him not to graduate. He was very confused by this. But he thought he might offend God if he graduated against the angel's instruction. Herschel told no one of his dream but delayed his graduation another term. By now he was very unsure of his future, which he and his family had planned and saved for.

One morning he opened his door to two Mormon missionaries who were tracting the street he lived on. He told them about rabbinical college. One elder showed Herschel a Book of Mormon, the paperback edition that was distributed several years ago. On the front cover of the book was a picture of the angel Moroni in the same pose as the gold-plated statue atop Mormon temples. When Herschel saw the picture of the angel Moroni he at once recognized the angel he had seen in his dreams. He immediately began studying The Book of Mormon. The missionaries taught him. He abandoned his *Talmudic* studies and was baptized into the Church soon thereafter. In his baptismal blessing he was told he was chosen to be a great missionary to the Jewish dead beyond the veil who were waiting for him to teach them.

A year after his baptism Herschel married in the temple. A year following that he was diagnosed with terminal cancer and died within six months. His wife is convinced he was called home by God after his baptism to fulfill his calling in the spirit world. Though she misses him terribly she never grieved for his death. She felt she knew he had a new calling and a new mission on the other side of the veil. We think of all the good and honorable Jews on the other side of the veil who were waiting for this man to teach them, for the Jews in the spirit world will have to be taught, also...

2.

What is it that drew this devout Jewish man away from his beloved *Talmud Torah*? What is it that drew me toward the church so strongly that I moved into a room with no running water, plumbing or heat, to investigate it?

I think it is the knowledge that the *Torah* and also the *Talmudic* writings are not complete in themselves. They do not claim to be. In fact, those *Torah* scholars who know their scriptures thoroughly will readily admit there is more knowledge that we must have to fully understand God's plan for his children on earth. Judaism does point the way to Christ because the next logical step after the Old Testament and the prophets is the fulfilling of the prophecies, the knowledge that all we have prepared ourselves to receive must soon become available to us. The Gospel of Jesus the Christ is the reward of those who seek answers to the questions of eternity. I know that sometime in the near future the Jewish people will be brought to their knees once again, this time in recognition of their Savior who waits for them; they will know their Shepherd at last.

Our Deliverer charts the growth of our spirits and welcomes us to Paradise at our return. That crystal fragment of God which we each carry within us is like a spiritual *liahona* (compass) in a force field of His unconditional love, guiding us home again. The vehicle we will use for our spiritual journey is the faith each of us builds.

3.

By the time I came to Betty and Dan's farm I had already been taught a little by two sets of missionaries, those from San Diego and Eugene. From these teachings I came to believe that religion is to be judged by its fruits. I think that the essential purpose of religion is to bring each of us to a feeling of inspirational oneness with our Heavenly Father, based upon our faith and knowledge of His eternal principles. Through these guidelines we may correctly know the love our Father has for us. We can love and serve Him in return, secure in the knowledge of who and what He is and how He operates in our lives. Dan says it this way:

" Jews don't have to be totally converted because they already know they are people of the covenant; their belief in God is so strong. Their *Torah* teaches correct principles. They just need to have all the information. They need to be added upon. Mormons are Hebrews, too, because they are from the tribes of Israel, just as the Jews are. We are all brothers." Christ himself, who was a Jew, came to tell us that, but few would listen. (See 2Ne chapters 25-30.)

I can tell those of the Jewish faith now about their ancient inheritance as it has been revealed to Joseph Smith. In The Book of Mormon, looking at the Savior's words in 3Ne 20:27, the ancient covenant the Lord made with Abraham is reiterated. We know that the covenant was reaffirmed to Isaac and Jacob. (See Gen 26:1-5, 24, Gen 28:1-4, 10-14) These promises are of transcendent significance. The main points of the covenant are these:

1. Abraham's posterity would be numerous. Abraham would become father of many nations.

2. Abraham's posterity is entitled to hold the priesthood and to have eternal increase. Through the priesthood the seed of Abraham will bless all nations.
3. Through Abraham's lineage would come Christ and other spiritual leaders.
4. The eternal inheritance includes certain lands or countries.
5. The covenant will be everlasting.

Some of these promises are to be fulfilled in coming years. When Christ visited America he again gave these transplanted Hebrews God's covenants, to confirm its promise and continuation. The Prophet Joseph Smith, also descended from the ancient lines of Jesse and Joseph, is the prophet who came to restore those promises in these times for all time. The Lord has remembered his covenant to the children of the house of Israel.

In my studies and prayers I asked to be shown the whole measure of God's kingdom. What could I hope for here on earth and afterward as a child of God? After all those miserable years I yearned for all the rights, blessings and gifts from God I could receive!

4.

After I was baptized I was asked to give a talk in a Sacrament meeting. I tried then to organize in my mind the major issues which kept me from joining the church for nine years after first receiving The Book of Mormon from my brother. For a long time these differences represented walls which kept the rest of the world out of my spiritual territory. Eventually, they became hurdles to climb over, then real problems that begged solving so I could progress. For almost a half century it never occured to me that there could be more than God, the nation of Israel, the *Torah*, the *Talmud*, the synagogue. These were sacred to me. I dared not read Christian (heretical) literature or seriously consider Christian things. Though I have always been a rebel with regard to many things, this was one area I demurred to my upbringing, unaware of how bound to it I was.

Following baptism I read and reread the scriptures, seeking to know each principle and to receive testimony of it. Though I had done this before revelation was given me I found it impossible to accept each concept without question. I always read with an anxiety of incompleteness, like a pilgrim entering a foreign but necessary land. Now I could read and believe Christian scripture, though I almost believed it earlier, if that makes any sense! As a new member of the Church I endeavored to discover everything all over again.

My first problem was, of course, a lifetime of not believing in Jesus Christ as the world's Messiah.  I did not know my Savior.  The Jewish people have turned aside the Holy Ghost.  They misinterpreted the prophecies of his coming to earth and do not recognize him as the *Mashiach*.  They had "blind guides." Matt 23:24

How do the Jewish people feel about Christianity and about Jesus in particular?  I remember my father telling me when very young that Christians have always hated Jews, that Jews have been maligned, tortured and even slaughtered by those of different beliefs, and usually those people professed to be Christian.  He would bring up the Holocaust as an example and he told me that if Jews had not been hated for practicing their religion they would not have been murdered.  He believed that Christians would again become the murderers of Jews if they were free to do so.

*The noted Jewish author and speaker, Elie Wiesel, has said:*

*"If I told you that I believe in God I would be lying.  If I told you that I did not believe in God I would be lying.  If I told you that I believe in man, I would be lying.  If I told you I did not believe in man I would be lying.  But one thing I do know: the Messiah has not come yet."*
*Shadows of Auschwitz, p. 161.  Quoted in Jewish Wisdom*

My mother simply called non-Jews *goyim*, as if they weren't of value. But later in her life I know she softened those views quite a bit and began to understand more of our purpose as sons and daughters of God.

What about the prophecy made by the Jews' beloved prophet Isaiah?

*Therefore the Lord himself shall give you a sign; Behold, a virgin shall conceive, and bear a son, and shall call his name Immanuel.  Butter and honey shall he eat, that he may know to refuse the evil, and choose the good.  Isa 7:14-15.*

Echoed again in Isa 8:8 and in Micah 5:2-3, this seems to be an unmistakable prophecy of Christ's birth into mortality.  For the Jews it should have been their first clue that the babe in Bethlehem had special, even royal significance.  How could they have overlooked it?  There are too many possibilities to explore in this book.

In the synagogue the *rabbi* explained things to me from the standpoint of *Torah*:

"In *Torah* the first commandment says we must have no other gods before our God, because our Jehovah (meaning God) is a jealous God.  Jesus cannot be

God's son, therefore, because he would be another god.  This goes against *Torah*'s teachings, (though the writers did not deal with the word *before*). Christianity *is* the fulfillment of Judaism.  Judaism, however, never claims to be complete in itself.  A Christian must be baptized to be 'saved', but a Jew belongs to the covenant made with Jehovah and believes he is automatically accepted by God as a disciple.  Remember Isaiah, our great prophet?  He talked about the survival of the Jews for thousands of years as a fulfillment of God's prophecy. We Jews believe this to be the voice of God speaking to us.  Look at Isaiah 43:2:3.

*When thou passest through the waters, I will be with thee,*
*And through the rivers they shall not overflow thee;*
*When thou walkest through the fire thou shalt not be burned*
*Neither shall the flame kindle upon thee,*
*For I am the Lord thy God, the Holy One of Israel, thy Savior.*
*Masoretic Text*

I don't mean to give the impression that Jews do not think a messiah is necessary.  Many passages in the *Talmud* are concerned with the arrival and ministry of this long awaited master teacher, called *Rabboni*.  When he appears the *shofar* (ram's horn), will be sounded to herald his arrival.  But the sages expected to see their *maschiach* riding a fine horse at the head of an army coming to rescue only the Jewish people from their enslavers.  The Jewish view of the expected *mashiach* is a romantic one and completely secular.  He would come to the Jews to instruct them further in the ways of God, to free them and to ensure their eternal safety and happiness.  He was not expected to change the Sabbath day nor to save all mankind, not to suffer and die on a cross for all people when God's covenant people were in such need of saving.

To Jews, Savior means God.  The *mashiach* would not claim to be the same Jehovah which the Jews have always ascribed to their Heavenly Father. The Jewish messiah would appear on the scene and reveal himself to the learned Jewish men of the time, declaring himself to be their long awaited Savior descended from the family of ancient King David through his patriarchal line. The Jewish messiah would be a mortal.  He would not be born of mortal and immortal parents.

Jewish theologians believe that when he reveals himself the *mashiach* will bring the perfect age, the end of time.  He heals, he cures, he rids the Jews of their ills and rebuilds their Temple.  The *rabbi*s long for him and await his Coming.  They point to the coming joy of Zion (Israel in this case) and use the parable of the bride and bridegroom.  The bridegroom is the messiah who will usher in a time of peace, the final and true age of fulfillment in the life of Israel, his bride.

But what responsibility do the Jews have before the messiah comes? Can they be a community which does not as one read and study *Torah*? Can they be disparate members or must they become as an academy where charity is their byword, where good deeds (*mishnas*) will redeem them so they will be worthy of a messiah? Sadly, in the opinion of some Jewish leaders the chosen people are not ready for their Redeemer. We must study and live *Torah* with exactitude to be worthy of the messianic advent.

These are some of the ideas I grew up with, though the feeling of modern Jewry toward Jesus is changing somewhat. Jews tend to associate the concept of Jesus the Christ with their feelings toward the Catholic church, lumping all Christian religions together as being largely alike, largely false, and largely unnecessary. They see Jesus as the icon of a pretender to the Jewish throne. Is it any wonder it took nine years, eight missionaries and an angel from Heaven to persuade me otherwise?

5.

Once safely inside my room on the farm I began reading the New Testament with new eyes. I read of Joseph and Mary of Nazareth who carried the unborn Son of God to Bethlehem where the ruler of heaven and earth was born in a manger. I read of Jesus' intelligence, his confounding of the *rabbis* in synagogue with his questions. I marvelled at his works, his wondrous love and miracles, his candor. Praying to Heavenly Father before beginning my reading each day I found my heart opening, my mind forming pictures of the times Jesus lived in. How he must have suffered us! I see Jesus now as the Jew he was then, serious, bent on fulfilling his mission, a man of integrity trained by holy angels, intent upon delivering the word of his Father to all who would listen.

I read the scripture wherein Jesus told Nicodemus he was the Christ. Nicodemus did not understand. Jesus also told the Samaritan woman at the well. She wondered if he had told her the truth, and then knew he had. He told the Samaritans. They did not listen. He told those attending the Feast of the Tabernacles in the synagogues that he was the Christ and they mocked him. They attempted to stone him when he told them: *"Before Abraham was, I am."* *John 8:58.*

He told me of his Father's love for me as I sat in the LDS chapel years earlier, knowing a Presence was there, but not seeing him. He was near me during the long trials of my life. Jesus was with me in my grief when my father took out his anger on me for so many years. Jesus was with me when my mother disappeared and later when my marriage ended so sorrowfully. He has comforted me during my lifelong pain of loneliness. He has comforted me in my childlessness. I did not know him then, but I always hoped one day he would come. Now, thanks to his patience and love I was finally finding him. I was learning so much, and as I read of him I began to love his perfect longsuffering, his amazing tolerance, his sweet, gentle, innocent life. How I cried as I cry now when I read these uplifting words that offer such great hope to all of us who yearn for the perfect peace Jesus offers us:

*Blessed are they that mourn: for they shall be comforted. Matt 5:4*

*Peace I leave with you, my peace I give unto you: not as the world giveth, give I unto you. Let not your heart be troubled, neither let it be afraid. John 14:27*

By the time I reached the final chapters of Matthew, Mark, Luke and John, reading about Jesus' final hours of agony and surrender in the Garden of Gethsemane and on the cross, I had accepted in my heart that he was indeed my Savior. His courage became my hope. His sorrow became my repentance. His great sacrifice became the basis of the life I lead. How I love my Savior for the supreme choice he made for me and for all of us. I could truly see that this was more than some general on a horse with armies come to free the Jews from their bondage, to magically wave away all evil and return the wayward Jews to their Israel.

This was no fake messiah who came to deceive and to lead men away from God. This man was and truly is all that his heritage made him and all that Heavenly Father could give him. Through his death and resurrection Jesus beckons each of us to join him and to partake once again of heavenly peace and joy. Jesus the Jew was a man of cosmic faith. He knew us. He knows us. He came to freely share with us his life, his knowledge, his faith, his hope, his perfect example, his great charity. Jesus Christ gave his life that we may all eternally live. He is the Son of God, heir to all things that God has and is. He is the Christ. Praise God! Jesus Christ is *Mashiach ben David*!

# Chapter Six

### The Tapestry Unfolds

1.

Once I had achieved a testimony that Jesus is the Christ through the Holy Ghost and through my own reading, it was much easier to appreciate the organization of his church. I was shown a chart in Gospel Principles which placed the apostles and prophets as the foundation of the Church, with Jesus Christ its chief cornerstone, with the remaining priesthood offices placed upon that platform.

I learned for the first time that revelation has always been a part of God's Church, whether received by ancient or modern prophets. That these prophets ordained and blessed others as a basic function of their priesthood authority, just as Jesus did, was an awakening for me because I was able to see the pattern of the Church working even in Old Testament times. As I learned about the first principles and ordinances of the Gospel I was able to put the organization of the Church into logical perspective. My conception of the lives of ancient prophets was greatly increased when viewed as part of church structure. I felt great sympathy for and much greater understanding of Moses on the mount as he received the Commandments, watching the unfolding of the preparatory Gospel to the Hebrews.

I more easily conceptualized the eternal nature and the spiritual impact of those ancient patriarchal blessings given by the prophets. (Genesis 48-49) I marveled that I would soon receive one, as did Joseph of old! How exciting to see evidence of the eternal Gospel working throughout human history!

I remembered the Jewish custom of setting out a cup of wine on *shabbat* (Friday evening services) for Elijah the great prophet, who is regarded as Israel's guardian. As a child I was taught that Elijah was taken to heaven through the agency of a fiery chariot (See 2Kings 2:11,12) but will return during the coming times of great struggles for the Jews with news of the advent of the *Mashiach*. How I long to tell the Jews who await him to remember this scripture from Malachi 4:5-6:

*Behold, I will send you Elijah the prophet before the coming of the great and dreadful day of the Lord: And he shall turn the heart of the fathers to the children, and the heart of the children to their fathers, lest I come and smite the earth with a curse.*

Now read with me the Latter-day scripture from Doctrine and Covenants 110:13-16:

*After this vision had closed, another great and glorious vision burst upon us; for Elijah the prophet, who was taken to heaven without tasting death, stood before us, and said: Behold, the time has fully come, which was spoken by the mouth of Malachi - testifying that he (Elijah) should be sent, before the great and dreadful day of the Lord comes - To turn the hearts of the fathers to the children, and the children to the fathers, lest the whole earth be smitten with a curse - Therefore, the keys of this dispensation are committed into your hands; and by this ye may know that the great and dreadful day of the Lord is near, even at the doors.*

He is come! There is no need to set out the cup! Elijah has returned, but to a modern prophet, with a great and urgent message from the Savior: We will all be resurrected and can be united with our families forever!

My eyes were opened when I read again in the Old Testament of the building of the First and Second Temples. Now I could appraise these stories with a discrimination based upon new knowledge of eternal ordinances performed in the reverent temples of the Lord.

I have increased insight of Jesus' words to his apostles when he taught them of heavenly things. How I longed to tell my *Zaydeh*, my mother and father and all my relatives so unaware of these great truths that I had "found" many answers to the mysteries that keep Jews from understanding God's Plan of Salvation.

*Surely the Lord God will do nothing, but he revealeth his secret unto his servants the prophets. Amos 3:7*

At that point it took little urging to convince me logically that the true Church had been restored to the earth, though I already knew it through revelation. It was reasonable to me that when our Redeemer returns he will continue to lead his Church on earth. To do that he would have to restore it through a modern prophet similar to Abraham and Moses whose earnest but hard lives, boundless enthusiasm for truth and total obedience to God prepared them for the wonderful and terrible tasks they undertook.

Joseph Smith was the modern day tool of the Lord in these final days who fulfilled the prophecy of Ezekiel. How I love reading of Ezekiel's revelation that the "sticks" of Judah and Joseph were to come together "to become one in thine hand" (Ezk 37:15-19), forever uniting the tribes of Joseph and Ephraim to share "one Lord, one faith, one baptism" (Eph 4:5). Reading his words and the scriptures revealed through him, it made sense that he was the chosen successor to that long line of Hebrew prophets who steadily and passionately pointed the way toward the coming Millennium. Seen in that light all the spiritual milestones throughout the history of mankind from Adam, our first earthly priesthood holder, to President Gordon B. Hinckley, current Prophet of the Church, have been necessary markers in the march through time toward Judgement Day...and beyond.

In the light of this revelation I really enjoyed the first section of the Doctrine and Covenants and Jesus proclaims himself the author of this revelation and says:

*"Search these commandments, for they are true and faithful, and the prophecies and promises which are in them shall all be fulfilled...whether by my own voice or by the voice of my servants, it is the same."* Doctrine and Covenants 1:37,38

I recall the day Betty gave me The Doctrine and Covenants for the first time. I opened to a section and read with great interest and surprise.

"Who wrote this," I asked incredulously, thinking of the *Talmud* and its many writers. Betty directed me to the Introduction page of the book which told me it was a holy book containing the revelations of Jesus Christ to the Prophet Joseph Smith and others.

"But they're clear. There is only one opinion here, unlike the questions and answers posed in the *Talmudic* writings. This is amazing!" It was Jesus in the temple all over again, confounding the *rabbis*. I loved it. Immediately I went to my room and read for five or six hours. In that short time I learned more than I had in years of trying to decipher the meanings in the *Talmud!*

2.

Of course the *Torah* is a complex document, rich in human history and spanning a great number of generations of people and events. To a Jew *Torah* is the image of the universe. It is mystical in its compilation because it is composed of God's word, as are latter-day scriptures. My grandfather would read with me. He brought to life the stories of the building of the First Temple in the wilderness, the sacrificing of animals, the laws regarding the cleanliness of the priesthood holders and their many responsibilities. I enjoyed hearing of the Hebrews wandering in the wilderness, finding rest where they could to worship and to bake *matzoh*, letting it harden on their backs as they hurried on, unaware that the bread they ate and the water they rationed were in similitude of the sacrament of Jesus Christ!

Reading the *Talmud*, on the other hand, is like being invited to a years long committee meeting with dozens of scholars. All have much to say. All their opinions are different, many brilliant, some mysterious, some very practical. The *rabbis* who wrote opinions on *Torah* teachings were very learned and quite intense in their determination to investigate the meaning of ancient laws, test interpretations of various verses, extract large scale propositions of portions of the text and make them into rituals of daily observance. But I always left my readings with confusion. I wanted true, clear answers to eternal questions more than how to light a candle, when to wash, how to eat, who is to be buried near whom or how unknowable God is to us.

Millions of Jews have used *Torah* and *Talmud* to lead their lives, for *Torah* teaches us. My mother followed *Torah* rules in preparing food, cleaning house, raising children and going to work. My father was obedient to the many counsels of the *Talmudic* sages when he installed linoleum and charged fair prices of his customers. I also am happy to have learned these things, but they did not teach me about revelation, the purpose of baptism, or how to understand God's Plan for us. That was the spiritual "meat" I was craving.

My paternal grandfather's death and funeral was a good illustration of how the *Talmud Torah* operates in Jewish lives. He died of the complications of heart disease while I was a teenager. Grandma and their children were suddenly referred to as *onen* (distressed). They were not to be comforted in any way at first, to allow them time to mourn. Jewish mourners of the dead are relieved of all religious duties including prayer, shaving and haircutting.

Ancient Jewish belief stipulates that their dead be committed to the ground within twenty-four hours, if possible, unembalmed, without autopsy, because of a belief that it is sacriligious to mutilate God's creation. However, there are times when the family sits with the dead before burial up to three days. My grandma appointed her family to watch the body at all times so that agents of the Adversary could not claim his soul. They lit candles, placed them at *Zaydeh*'s head, an ancient practice meant to ward off evil spirits. Jews do believe a soul is immortal. If the dead was righteous death becomes an atonement for those left behind because death is considered a punishment for a life of sin. I recall my *rabbi* teaching that mankind could not live forever because of Adam's sin in the Garden.

After *Zaydeh*'s death the *Tziduk Ha-din* prayer was recited. A bucket of water was overturned outside his home:   In this way his death was communicated through the neighborhood without it being mentioned, supposedly keeping the Adversary (Satan) away from the eternal soul. *Zaydeh* was carefully and thoroughly washed by my grandmother and a helper, after which he was dressed in his good suit. (Old Hebrew tradition is to wrap the dead in shrouds, that is, wrappings in lieu of clothing.) *Zaydeh*'s *talit* (prayer shawl) that he put on before praying, was put on him, a piece of fringe being first cut off, in accordance with tradition, to release him from Jewish law. He was placed in a simple pine box (so his remains could quickly return to the earth) which was purchased by his five children. They buried him the next morning.

Once the burial casket has been sealed it is never opened again. My family was greatly grieved. They rent their clothing upon learning of the death, even before mourning began. This is a common practice among Jewish mourners, but in modern Jewry the wearing of black ribbons is usually substituted. I was greatly bereaved for my precious *Zaydeh*. I tore part of my hem off, trying to make a vertical tear in it. My mom got very angry at that!

At the gravesite the *rabbi* recited the *Kaddish* prayer, which begins "*Yit-gadal, ve yet kadash, shmay rabba...*" meaning "Glorified and sanctified by God's great name..." This great prayer in addition to the *Shema* is a Jew's way of informing God and those left behind that the dead has left life as a Jew. A *minyan* is required if the *Kaddish* is said at a public prayer service. There are many rules regulating the saying of the *Kaddish*, but I only remember grieving for my grandfather, then sitting *Shiva* (sitting with the dead three days) for him right after the internment. Being suddenly faced with the death of a loved one when we had no clue as to his spirit's place of rest was very difficult for all of us.

Superstition plays a large part in Jewish rituals of birth, marriage and death. When my mother wanted to take some of *Zaydeh*'s things from his house my grandmother was angry and refused her. She said it would disturb the *tuma,* the spirit of uncleanness and impurity which permeates a house of mourning. She was afraid the *tuma* would spread to our house.

For a year afterward it seemed no one spoke of my grandfather without also saying the words *alav ha-shalom* (may he rest in peace). *Zaydeh* was a vital man. His illness and death depressed all who knew him. They used to say to him "May you live to be one hundred and twenty," referring to Deut 34:7 which tells about Moses not dying before he reached that age. I believed that my grandfather would have lived at least that long!

My family grieved for *Zaydeh* twelve months. They and many friends sat

*Shiva* for him for thirty days, as is the custom. At the end of this mourning period a *Kaddish* prayer was again said for him. It seemed we mourned him for years, recalling the tears we shed during our prayers or listening to Grandma cry at night. We didn't go to the movies or have any outside fun. Friends were sometimes invited to come sit *Shiva* with us, but we were forbidden from having a good time together. I could not get over *Zaydeh*'s death and disappearance from our lives. Where was Grandpa? Only God knew. We knew only that this life was over for him and that he dwelt somewhere in something called vaguely "the hereafter."

Even in synagogue the reminder of his life and death was constantly there. Grandma bought a light in the synagogue for *Zaydeh*. Every year on the anniversary of his death that light was turned on. Friday nights a *yahrzeit* (yartz-hight), a prayer for the dead, was recited. Even after years had passed we still cried for *Zaydeh* when the *yahrzeit* was read with the Mourner's *Kaddish*, which my father sometimes recited.

*O Lord, what is a man that you are mindful of him. Man is like a breath, his days like a passing shadow. In the morning he flourishes and grows up like grass. In the evening he is cut down and withers. So teach us to number our days. That we may get us a heart of wisdom. Mark the man of integrity, and behold the upright, for there is a future for the man of peace.*
*Selections from Psalms and Ecclesiastes adapted from The Jewish Mourner's Book of Why, p. 349.*

In Judaism the individual is of greatest importance. The *Talmud* states that God originally created only Adam, so if he had been killed, humanity would have been destroyed. As it is, all can be saved. Many implications can be taken from this idea. We can all say "For my sake the world was created." *(Mishna Sanhedrin 4:5)*. A Yiddish proverb says: "If I try to be like him, who will be like me?" A *Hasidic rabbi* strongly believed that personality is unique, so much so that no one should alter himself to please the person being spoken to:

*"If I am because I am I, then I am I and you are you. But if I am I because you are you, and you are you because I am I, then I am not I and you are not you."*
*Quoted in Jewish Wisdom)*

How grateful I am for the knowledge of Jesus Christ who taught mankind of the resurrection of all souls from the dead! Because of this I no longer look at death as a great mystery. No longer do I worry about *Zaydeh*. I know he is happy where he is.

Unfortunately, the Jewish theory of the resurrection of the dead is quite limited, perhaps because the *Torah* makes no references to it, other than the vision of Ezekiel (See Ez 37). In the second century b.c.e. the Sadducees and the Pharisees discussed it, with the result that they split the vote on accepting it as doctrine. The *rabbis* accepted the belief, so they know the soul lives after death of the body, but there is only speculation on what the "afterlife" holds. These ruminations occupy some of the *Kabbalah* text.

3.

Actually, Jewish literature is full of wonderful stories and sayings based upon the *Talmud Torah*. Many aspects of Judaism are similar in philosophy to those of Latter-day Saints.

**Giving and Receiving**
Biblical law forbids taking interest on all loans. Loans given for the purchase of necessities cannot have interest added. To those trying to avoid going on welfare, *Gemakh* (Free Loan Society) societies have existed throughout history. Jewish tradition encourages one and all to try all options before asking for charity or welfare. Those at poverty levels of living are also encouraged to give charity and to care for the poor, so none will feel helpless or without agency. Those who have much are commanded to be generous. Honest accumulation of wealth is okay but charity must be in appropriate measure. *Rabbi Akiva* long ago said that through our charity to the poor we may be saved in the world to come.

*The merit of fasting is the charity (dispensed).*
*Quoted in Jewish Wisdom, p. 17. From the Babylonian Talmud*

Sometimes *Torah* teachings seem to make it hard to know whether to ask for help.

*In a 19th century Russian town a wealthy man lost all he had. Greatly ashamed, he told no one, soon dying of malnutrition. The town rabbi told the townspeople who were ashamed that the man suffered from excessive pride. He should have asked for help and admitted his situation.*
*From the Babylonian Talmud. Quoted in Jewish Wisdom*

My uncle once told me about a poor man who asked him for clothes. My uncle, seeing that the man wore rags, wondered if he had better clothes at home and gave him nothing. "Then the man asked for food," said my uncle. "I took him in and fed him, so he wouldn't die while we were talking."

**Visiting and Helping the Sick**
*Rabbi Akiva's* student became sick but no one visited him, so the *rabbi*

went to him. He cleaned the sick man's home. The student recovered and said "You have given me life!" The *rabbi* taught "Those who do not visit the sick might as well have spilled their blood."

## Honesty and Dishonesty

I am reminded of the wisdom I was given in synagogue about the choices I would have to make between lying and telling the truth. It was told to me that I should live my life as if every act was recorded in a book by someone who sees and hears everything. Whenever I wanted to do wrong I should think that if I were asked what I was doing I could say "I'm shoplifting" and be jailed or I could lie and violate the commandments. In this way I could stay moral and have a perfect repentance.

My father was an honest man in dealing with everyone. I have tried to be the same way, following his example. He charged less than other contractors but did faultless work, saving his customers as much money as he could and telling them how he did it. He never bought cheap material to save cost when quality would have saved them money in the long run. These things he learned from his father who learned it from his father. They all studied *Torah*.

*The shopkeeper must wipe his measures twice a week, his weights once a week, and his scales after every weighing.  Mishna Bava Bathra 5:10*

If a Jew robs a Jew he violates biblical law, but it is worse for him if he robs a non-Jew. Then he disgraces his people and his religion. My father told me that many times when I accompanied him on jobs. This sage advice comes from the *Tosefta* commentary somewhere in *Talmud*. Jewish law states that each of us is responsible for the consequences which come from our actions.

My grandfather had several old *Talmud*s with all the commentaries. This is from the section on Laws of Murder and Preservation of Life:

It is forbidden to sell weapons of war to the immoral. We cannot help them in any way by selling them anything which can endanger the public. But we can sell them shields for their own defense.

"By the same token, Israel," my grandmother chimed in, "Don't ask your brother to eat with you if you know he won't, and don't give him bets on horses if you know he shouldn't gamble."

## Healthfulness

Jews are very concerned with health, but they do not boast about it, lest evil spirits hear and upset things. My uncle was a funny man who loved to tell jokes. When we went on trips he would wish us well, saying "*Sholem aleichem* (health be with you). Have a good trip. If you get sick, God forbid, may you do it in the best of health!"

## Wisdom

Two people fought over a piece of land, each claiming it belonged to him. A *rabbi* was brought to decide. He could not come to terms, either. "Let us ask the land itself," he decided. Putting his ear to the ground the *rabbi* listened and then stood up and proclaimed "My friends, the land says it belongs to neither of you - you belong to it."
(Traditional folktale adapted from David Stein's A Garden of Choice Fruit: 200 Classic Jewish Quotes, p.54.)

## Conversion

There is the story of the two leading *rabbi*s long ago who met a heathen who said "Convert me to Judaism on condition that you teach me the whole *Torah* while I stand on one foot." One *rabbi* chased him away but the heathen came before the second *rabbi* who converted him, saying "What is hateful to you do not unto your neighbor. This is the whole *Torah*. The rest is commentary. Now go and study."
(Babylonian *Talmud, Shabbat* 31a. Quoted in Jewish Wisdom)

A more sobering wisdom is found in the Jewish conception of life after this life. From the Babylonian *Talmud*, this extract:

*In the World-to-Come, there will be no eating, or drinking, or procreation, or business, or jealousy or hatred or competition, but the rightous will sit with crowns on their heads feasting on the radiance of the shekinah (sheck in ah), the divine presence. Berakhot 17a*

Though doubts about an "afterlife" are very common among Jews I maintain great hope that the Spirit of the Lord will continue to suffer with them until they come to realize, as I did, that Jesus is the Christ, and that the wondrous *shekinah* they all seek is but a prayer away. Now I know that the Eternal Light is truly the Light of Christ, which is given to all people. Jesus Christ is the light and the life of the world, in part because he came as a prophet to deliver the truth as his Father gave it to him. One day the Jews will come to realize that. Meanwhile, he longs for them and with great hope awaits their knock.

# Chapter Seven

No Beginning and No End

In a dream recently I was aware of a voice which awoke me with these words. I will share them with you.

*"God is supreme in the universes. He is without parallel or equal in the courts on high. His Son, Jesus Christ, is the creator of this and other worlds. He is the eternal Son of God. He is our Mediator with the Father, our brother, our friend, our Judge, our Advocate with the Father, our Redeemer and our Savior. He regulates and handles the welfare of us all. There is nothing he does not know or do. He has been to earth many thousands of times, as this is his world as well as Satan's paradise. We, his creation, are saved through Christ's atoning blood which was shed for us all that we may dwell with the Father in Heaven once again in glory.*

*The Church of Jesus Christ of Latter-day Saints is true. It reigns above all that has ever been and is on the earth today in preparation for the Second Coming of Jesus Christ which is coming soon, sooner that we suspect, and we will all be judged by our Perfect Judge and Redeemer.*

*Those readers who come to understand the truth of The Book of Mormon and the other Standard works will be especially blessed in the spirit world with great blessings of family and children. They will endure forever in the sight of the eternal God and His righteous, perfect kingdom.*

*Joseph Smith was a perfect man on earth in his time. Those who love and understand him will reap great blessings of understanding and love of the scriptures. He gave his life for you. He is here with us now and he is happy. He is teaching the Gospel now to those in the spirit world who would not or who did not hear it in life. In the name of Jesus Christ, amen."*

My life since my baptism has not been without problems, but I know the truth now. I understand that we are given trials to strengthen us. The Lord allows us to choose between good and evil, between what is right for us and what is not. He has not left us alone, but has given us a prophet to guide us, scriptures to teach us, righteous members of His priesthood to bestow his blessings upon us. He has given us many ways of getting the help we need. We have the great blessing of repentance and His forgiveness, which allows us to reach again for the best within ourselves that we may present a stainless life to our Eternal Father. He gives us every good thing in accordance with the choices we made in the pre-existence.

I am grateful for the light I have found as a Christian and as a member of The Church of Jesus Christ of Latter-day Saints. It is a frightening thought that I might have turned Christianity aside for the remainder of my time in this life, never allowing myself the experience of knowing joy through loving my Savior, had not others persuaded me to explore the full Gospel.

There is so much we do know that helps us to understand our purposes here and our rewards hereafter. We must continue to learn His ways, and the ways of the Great Martyr, else we perish in ignorance. I remember the uplifting ending of Victor Hugo's great novel *"Les Miserables"* where the hero, Jean Valjean speaks for the final time:

*"(God) is on high, he sees us all, and he knows what he does in the midst of the great stars... Love each other dearly always. There is scarcely anything else in the world but that..." (p.333)*

My gratitude to Heavenly Father and to Jesus Christ is very great. To show my thankfulness for learning of Christ and wanting to live his truths I willingly and happily dedicate my life to my Lord, my God. He has blessed me beyond all deserving, as a Jew and as a Christian.

I am so happy I have discovered that truly Jesus is the Christ and that he paid for our individual sins with his Atonement if we repent. I feel that I finally begin to comprehend the amazing vision of the true future of mankind.

I never knew that opportunity existed until I heard the full Gospel and came to know The Book of Mormon is true. To turn from the Lord, to deny him invites loneliness, pleases the Adversary and ensures a trouble-filled life.

The tapestry of eternity is always unfolding. From Adam in the Garden through the Law of Moses, through the life and ministry of Jesus Christ and the ensuing Great Apostasy following the death of the Christ's apostles, to the restoration of the original Church of Jesus Christ. The unrolling of the Plan of our Heavenly Father is moving with divine logic and perfect certainty toward the inevitable Judgement Day. Zion is within us and before us, always in reach.

I have spoken to a number of people who truly believe our church is temporary and will not withstand time. To them I mention that there are over 52 temples in twenty-nine countries. The Book of Mormon has been translated into at least 88 languages including ASL and Braille. Others are always in the works.

At present there are more than 50,000 full time missionaries in the field. People in all countries are accepting the Gospel all the time. This is an international church. The Lord has said that this is His Church and that it will go forward until it covers the earth. (See Doctrine and Covenants, Section 1)

One beautiful day the Gospel will be preached in Israel.

*Wherefore, seek not the things of this world but seek ye first to build up the kingdom of God, and to establish his righteousness...*
*Joseph Smith Translation, Matthew 6:38*

What else really matters?

## Song of Redeeming Love

Heavenly Father, Thou with whom seraphs abide,
Come, lift our spirits with Thy flame of lasting love,
Thy perfect grace.
That all who enter in Thy care may see again
Thy sacred Face.

O, may our souls be giv'n unto
Eternal joy and peace.
Thy grace abounds.  Thy mercy swells
the hearts of all who hear Thy call.

The sweetest melody of all.
Thy wondrous song of Redeeming love.

Marlena Tanya Muchnick

# Appendix One

THE STICK OF JUDAH AND THE STICK OF JOSEPH

2000 bce - 1996 bce    *Abram (Abraham)

1996 – 1836 bce    *Isaac

*Jacob (Israel)

Reuben, Simeon, Levi, Judah, Dan, Naphtali, Gad, Asher, Assachar, Zebulon, Joseph, Benjamin,
(Manasseh, Ephraim - sons of Joseph.   Received Reuben's birthright which he lost because of transgression. See 1Chron 5:1,2)

House of Israel

Moses

Reign of Judges

1095 bce    Saul annointed king
1063 bce    David annointed king
1015 bce    Solomon annointed king

975 bce    Ten tribes revolt, form  separate entity, Kingdom of Israel
Kingdom of Judah retains tribes of Judah and Benjamin

circa 721 bce    Captives carried to the North by the Assyrians
became the Ten Lost Tribes

606-585 bce    Hebrews carried captives by the Babylonians

600 bce    Lehi leaves for America

*5 bce- 1 bce    **Birth of Christ

ce 34    Nephites and Lamanites
Visit of Jesus (See The Book of Mormon 3Ne 11)

* Dates in dispute among scholars

ce 70          Jerusalem destroyed
               Jews scattered

ce 421         Nephite nation destroyed
               Lamanite nation continues

ce 1830        Bible and The Book of Mormon come together in the restoration of the
               Gospel.

**Taken from "The Mortal Messiah
   *from Bethlehem to Calvary*" Note 2, pp. 349-350
Bruce R. McConkie
Deseret Book Company
Salt Lake City, Utah 1979

This Appendix is partly from
The Holy Bible
Published by The Church of Jesus Christ of Latter-day Saints
1987 Edition

also from
Book of Mormon Student Manual
Religion 121-122, Second Edition Revised 1981
The Church of Jesus Christ of Latter-day Saints,
Salt Lake City, Utah
Used by permission

# Appendix Two

PROPHECIES OF THE SAVIOR IN THE OLD TESTAMENT

LINEAGE, DIVINE BIRTH AND YOUTH

| | |
|---|---|
| Genesis 49:9,10 | Of the tribe of Judah |
| Psalms 2:7 | The Father acknowledges him to be His Son |
| Isaiah 7:14; 9:16-7 | Born of a virgin, place of birth, lineage of David |
| 11:1,10; 53:2; 60:6 | Lineage, grow as plant, the Magi (Matt 2:11) |
| Jeremiah 23:5,6 | Of the house of David |
| 31:15,; 33:15 | Massacre of innocents, lineage (Matt 2:18) |
| Daniel 3:25; 7:13 | References to the Son of God |
| Hosea 11:1 | Taken for refuge into Egypt (Matt 2:15) |
| Micah 5:2,3 | Relation to God, of tribe of Judah, born in Bethlehem |

MORTAL MINISTRY

| | |
|---|---|
| Deut 18:15-19 | Advent, prophet |
| Psalms 8:2; 35:11 | Triumphant entry, condemnation |
| 41:9; 45:1-17 | Betrayal by friend, characteristics of life and work |
| 56:1-6; 69:8-9 | Presence of enemies, disbelief of brethren, temple cleansin |
| 71:10-11; 72:1-20 | Plots against Christ, his life and work |
| 78:2; 110:1-4 | Teaching, parables, his life and work |
| 118:22-23, 26 | Rejected of men, acclamations on; entry in Jerusalem |
| Proverbs 8:32-36 | His teachings |
| Isaiah 6:9-10; 8:14 | Rejected teachings, rejected of men to Jews |
| 9:1; 11:1-3; 28:16 | Place of ministry, life and work, cornerstone |
| 40:3; 9-11; 42:1-5 | Herald goes before him, time of advent, persecution |
| 49:7; 50:4-9; 52:13-15 | Persecution, his life and work |
| 53:1-3; 61:1-2 | His life and work, teachings |
| Jeremiah 7:11 | Desecration and cleansing of temple |
| Zechariah 9:9; 11:12-13 | Triumphal entry to Jerusalem, betrayal |
| Exodus 12:1-14; 46 | Lamb of God, bones not broken |
| Leviticus 16:7-22 | Sin offering in behalf of people |
| Numbers 21:6-9 | Brass serpent lifted on pole to save people |
| Job 19:25 | Reference to Redeemer |
| Psalms 22:1-19; 31:4-5 | Suffering and crucifixion |
| 34:20; 35:11; 41:9 | No bone broken, condemnation, betrayal |
| 69:9,21; 109:21-26` | Mocked, his sufferings |
| 118:22,23 | Rejected of men |
| Isaiah 8:14,15; 49:7-8 | Rejected of men, stumbling stone, mediator |

| 52:3, 4-12; 59:16 | Suffering, atonement, death, intercessor provided |
| 63:3 | Blood of others upon him |
| Daniel 9:24-26 | Cut off, vicarious sacrifice |
| Hosea 13:4,14 | Savior, Redeemer and Ransomer |
| Zechariah 11:12,13 | Betrayal by friend and disciple |
| 12:10; 13:6-7 | Pierced, betrayed |


## RESURRECTION, TRIUMPH AND DIVINITY

| Genesis 1:1 | Called the Word of God (Ps 33:6, Jn 1:1-14) |
| 2 Samuel 7:12 | King of Israel |
| Job 19:25 | To stand upon the earth |
| Psalms 2:6-8; 8:4-6 | Exaltation, Son of Man, supremacy |
| 16:10-11; 17:15 | Resurrection |
| 45:17; 56:13; 68:18 | Name eternal, resurrection, ascension, triumph |
| 72:17; 89:27; 110:1-3 | Name eternal, firstborn, King of Kings, exaltation |
| 110:4-7; 118: 17-19 | Resurrection and triumph |
| Proverbs 8:22-31 | Foreordination and divinity |
| Isaiah 9:6-7; 11:2-5 | Mighty God, kingdom, supremacy |
| 45:23; 53:10; 61: 1-3 | Ultimate universal acceptance, immortality, kindness, power |
| Daniel 7:13-14 | Son of man to have everlasting dominion |
| Hosea 13:14 | To destroy death |
| Jonah 1:17 | Raised on third day (Matt 16:4) |
| Malachi 4:1-2 | Second Advent foretold |

The Life and Teachings of Jesus and His Apostles
Course Manual, Second Edition
The Church of Jesus Christ of Latter-day Saints, 1979
Salt Lake City, Utah
Adapted with permission

# Appendix Three

### EVIDENCES OF THE
### TRUE CHURCH

*The following conditions, as specified in the Holy Scriptures, must exist for a church to qualify as the true Church Jesus the Christ established when He was here upon the earth.*

1.  Will recognize the Holy Trinity as separate Persons.
    a) Will know identity of God (Father), Jesus Christ (Son) and the Holy Ghost (Spirit).

2.  Will accept the Holy Bible in its entirety.
    a) Will recognize that some parts of the record are missing.

3.  Will contain the same offices.
    a) 12 Apostles mandatory.
    b) Prophets, Teachers, Elders, Evangelists, Bishops, Deacons High Priests, Saints.

4.  Officers will be "Called of God."
    a. College Degree or license insufficient
    b. Royal Priesthood.
    c. Can be married.

5.  Will have an unpaid Ministry.

6.  Members will be workers in Church.
    a. Women included in activities

7.  Baptism will be mandatory.
    a. Probably "down in water."

8.  Will believe in the Virgin Birth.

9.  Will believe in a literal resurrection.

10. Will honor Sunday as the Sabbath.

11. Will receive continuous revelation.

12. Will be payors of tithes.

13.         Will partake in the Sacrament of the Lord.

14.         Will believe in immortality and Heaven and a Hell.

15.         Will have miraculous occurrences.
            a. Healings, visions, tongues, prophecies.

16.         Will teach that Jesus Christ will come again.

17.         Will be persecuted for beliefs.

"Shortly after the beginning of World War II, Floyd Weston and four of his college friends set out on a quest to find the one true church of Jesus Christ. Armed with a list of 17 points they had compiled out of the New Testament, they began visiting different churches searching for the one church that matched the Church the Savior had established while he was in the Holy Land.

Although separated by service in the Armed Forces, in the next few years four of the five young men, by differing routes and under varying circumstances, independently found the one church that incorporated the entire 17 points. The fifth was unable to join because he had been killed in an air crash." Floyd Weston

Appendix used by permission of Floyd Weston
and is reprinted as he instructed.

# Glossary of Terms

### B.C.E.

This annotation means "before the common era." Because Jews do not accept Jesus as the Christ they do not use the annotations B.C. (before Christ) or A.D. (year of our Lord).

### Diaspora

The dispersion or exile of the Hebrews into the lands outside of Israel and Judah, after the Babylonian captivity. Exile refers to an involuntary exodus, as during the Persian conquest of Babylon. When the Babylonian king allowed the Jews to return to Palestine, many refused because they had become acclimated to that alien culture. Those people who remained in a country not their own while assimilating into it lived in *diaspora*.

The reality of *diaspora* has had great impact on the *Talmud* because people from all over the world living in *diaspora* countries wanted to know how to adapt *Torah* teachings to their country's habits and laws. They wrote their *rabbis* asking for advice. These writings in part became part of *Torah* commentary. Jews not living in Israel are living in *diaspora*.

### Hasidim

Pronounced *ha seed im,* the word means a pious man, a disciple of a great *rabbi.* During the 18th century in central and eastern Europe this movement was very popular. It was started by a mystic named Israel ben Eliezer. He was a wanderer, preaching a gospel that made him very popular among the common folk of the time. He sang the praises of simple faith, everyday pleasures, worship in a state of joy, in opposition to the strict rabbinical teachings. They teach celebration of God in a warm, personal way. The movement still exists in larger cities.

### Hebrew

The name comes from the time of Abraham who lived east of the Tigris and Euphrates rivers in the Chaldean wilderness of the old Assyrian empire. His tribe of wanderers were referred to as Eber, meaning "people of the other side." The word evolved into the current "Hebrew." Hebrews are a distinctive people, claiming descent from Abraham, Isaac and Jacob. Since the *Diaspora* they have intermarried with most of the world's peoples and have lost the racial characteristics and traceable genealogy. Those who returned to Palestine after the Babylonian captivity were primarily of the tribe of Judah and some from the tribe of Benjamin and are presently identified as the Jewish people.

## Jew

Other than the practicing of Judaism as a convert, a Jew claims descent from ancient tribes of Hebrew people, often called Israelites. "The name indicates, first of all, a man from the kingdom of Judah." (LDS Bible Dictionary, p. 713). Because to be Jewish means to be of Semitic origin, Jews are not descended from the white race, though through the millenia they have intermarried with most races. This feeling of ancient separateness often contributes to their secularism.

1. Orthodox Jewry
A traditional approach to Judaism based upon the laws of commandments. The holy observances revealed by God in *Torah* - the Law of Moses. Orthodox Jews are the most fundamental group. All prayers and readings are in Hebrew. To live by *Torah* as interpreted by the writers of the *Talmud* is the wish and practice of this rigid and ultraconservative original Jewish movement. A variation, *Hasidim* (pious) contains mystical overtones regarding God and the scriptures. Members of this the original sect believe a religion wherein joy and emotional experiences are of primary import in Jewry. *Torah* is the supreme authority. *Yarmulkes* (skull caps) are always worn and tithing is paid.

2. Conservative Jewry
Conservative congregations have a somewhat progressive attitude toward religious observation. Hats are still worn in synagogue. Tithing is encouraged and holy days are observed. Services are held in Hebrew and English. Jewish celebrations and customs are not rigidly observed because members are responsive to needs of a modern society.

3. Reform Jewry
This group of Jews are the most progressive in that Hebrew is used primarily only in reading *Torah*. Hats are not worn in synagogue. Services are held in English with Hebrew available for reading. Modern *rabbis* and *cantors* include women. Commandments are of course observed, as are ceremonies and customs but these may change accordingly as conditions change from place to place. Reform congregations stress the Hebrew language and do not deny the values taught by the mystical work, the *Kabbalah* (see below). Originating in Germany by governments which tried to convert the Jews, the movement failed. Nonetheless, Reform Jewry does not strictly adhere to ancient biblical teachings. All mainstream Jewish congregations support Zionism.

## Kabbalah

This kind of esoteric thought began with an elect group of scholars deeply involved in psychic experience. Indian, Persian and Greek writings became involved with Jewish theories of emanation of spirits which served God as intermediaries to the physical world. Gradually, ideas of demons, angels and the spirit worlds themselves took shape in the writings of ancient mystics. There are stories of bad luck which befell several early *rabbinic* scholars who investigated heavenly mysteries but the *Kabbalah* blossomed among the Jews of Europe nonetheless. The mass of Jews of today are unfamiliar with this type of literature.

The diverse ideals of *Kabbalism* eventually became united in a book called *Sefar haZohar* (book of splendor), imposing a structure and a unified system giving descriptions and commentaries upon the Pentateuch. It contains Rabbi Isaac Luria's complex system of magic words and mystic exercises, diagrams of the *sephirot* (emanations) which are believed to mediate our earth from heaven, numerology as applied to the alphabet of the Hebrew language, some constellation astrology, the seven levels of heaven, mystic ideas of creation, codes, formulas and psychism. It is a serious work but not for the casual researcher or the hurried. Some of the questions posed in this work are answered by latter-day scripture!

## Keria

Literally means "tearing." When a Jewish funeral is held a garment must be rent as a sign of mourning. This can be done when the news is received or later in the house of *Shiva*, or at the cemetary before burial. It is usually started with a knife and torn further by hand. For a parent a *keria* is made on the left side, for others the right side is used. Normally a special garment is worn or used. *Keria* is never performed on the Sabbath or festivals but may be on some days of Passover and *Sukkot.*

## Kosher

When food is cooked or prepared according to Jewish dietary laws it is said to be *kosher.* It is a Yiddish word. Eating *kosher* food makes one stronger in devotion to God. Examples: milk and meat are not eaten at the same time. This comes from Moses' words in Exodus and Deuteronomy forbidding the people to seethe a kid in its mother's milk.

Only four footed animals that chew a cud and have cloven hooves are *kosher*. Crawling animals are forbidden. Fish must have scales and fins to be *kosher*. An animal that has not been slaughtered according to biblical ritual is unclean is *trayf* or non-*kosher*. Meat can only be declared *kosher* by a special supervisor.

## Offerings Under Mosaic Law

Burnt Offerings         Includes oxen, goats, sheep, doves or young pigeons. Must be male and without blemish. Symbolic of total surrender to God.

Peace Offerings         Can be male or female, without blemish. Cattle, sheep, goats. No fowl. To thank God or involving covenants or vows.

Sin Offerings         Male or female animals or fowl, without blemish. Made to atone for offenses against others or broken covenants. These offerings include extra offering for restitution against another.

## Pesach

A Jewish celebration of the liberation of Israel from Egyptian slavery. National birthday of Jews, occuring in March and April each year. Passover is also a celebration of nature's harvest. *Pesach* (or Passover) is significant of justice and of the inalienable rights given of God, celebration life and societal cooperation. These rights must be in tune with God, under His direction (See Num 15:40-41, Lev 19:33-36). When Moses led the Israelites from Egypt they had been under the yoke of slavery which Pharoah Ramses II imposed upon them. The Jews were not harmed by the plagues. After ten plagues were brought upon the Egyptian people, Ramses let the Israelites leave Egypt.

The *Torah* ordains that this feast of *Pesach* is to be celebrated for seven days. On the first night a lamb was sacrificed in the ancient Temple, consumed with *matzoh* (unleavened bread) and bitter herbs, to symbolize slavery and the hasty departure from bondage. Roasted lamb is no longer eaten. The events of the Exodus are sometimes reenacted (See Ex 12:26; 13:8, Deut 6:20). Special dishes and other ware are set for these nights. They are not used during the remainder of the year. Many dietary rules attend this holiday which involve *koshe*ring of food and utensils. Jews are commanded to use only unleavened bread, to make a traditional *seder* plate containing foods commemorative of the Exodus story. I recall many Passover *seders* in our family when we could put aside our differences, eat the traditional foods, say the required prayers and remember the great story of the Exodus.

## Rosh Hashanah

The start of the Jewish New Year. It is a time of self-examination, repentance, atonement. During this time of personal inventory we measure ourselves against what we know we ought to be and strive to make greater effort. The Orthodox believe it is the time of Heavenly Judgement.

*Rosh Hashanah* begins in the month of *Tishri*, the seventh month, the most important because of the significance of the number seven, meaning completeness. Usually a *shofar,* the ram's horn, is blown on this holiday. The *shofar* calls Jews to their special occasions. We greet each other with the words *L'Shanah tovah tiku sayvu.* (May you have a good year). Sweet food is served at dinner in the hope of a sweet, happy new year.

## Semites

Reading Genesis 10 informs us that of Noah's three sons, Shem, Ham and Japheth, Shem was the forerunner of the Semitic races. Japheth was progenitor of what is now known as the Indo-European family of nations, whereas Ham begat the dark-skinned races. The Semitic people originated in SW Asia and also include Sumerians, Phoenicians and Arabs. They are essentially an Asiatic race.

## Sephardim

Derived from the word "Spain." When in 1492 Jews living in Spain and Portugal were being forced to convert to Christianity or leave the country they chose to migrate to Turkey, Holland and Italy and further to the north. There are large Sephardic communities around the world. Many live also in Israel, North Africa and Turkey as well as in our larger cities.

## Shiva

The seven day mourning period for the dead (See Gen 50:10). It is courteous for friends of the deceased not to pay a call to the family the first three days following a death, as they will want to be alone in their mourning to "sit *Shiva*," to sit with the body or in honor of the dead. The first three days are obligatory, beginning immediately after interment. A lighted candle is put in the room near the head of the deceased.

In olden times the body was wrapped or draped and left in the room with the mourning family for three days. One purpose of forced mourning is to emphasize the difference between life and death, thereby increasing appreciation of life.

## Torah

The Pentateuch: Biblical books of Genesis, Exodus, Leviticus, Numbers and Deuteronomy as well as the Prophets section. The *Torah* (teaching) scroll is made of parchment. Every ark in every synagogue in the world has one. The men who write the *Torah* scroll feel they are given by God a holy calling to this lifelong work. They must do it perfectly. No errors are permitted. In an important way the *Torah* embodies the revelations of God, the teachings of prophets and *rabbi*s throughout the centuries. *Rabbi*s must be masters of *Torah* and its 613 commandments which are the essence of Judaic teachings.

*Torah* also includes the *Talmud*; in fact, all religious teachings of Judaism, which declares its creed: "God, *Torah*, Israel." In Paradise the righteous sit and study *Torah* all day, it is said. The prophet Ezra was said to be instrumental in establishing *Torah* as the law of Jewish life. He read it to the assembled Hebrews and the tradition has carried on with readings by *rabbi*s and congregation to each other. It was once chanted in Hebrew but translated into Aramaic. *Torah* needs to be read and translated, but is usually not translated.

There are really two *Torah*s, the Palestinian and the Babylonian. Each is composed of two sections, the *Mishnah*, a rabbinical commentary on the *Torah*, and the *Gemara*, a rabbinical commentary on the *Mishnah*. Each book deals with different tractates and each is from antiquity.

## Viddui

A confession of sins. When on the verge of death a person is urged to confess all sins. This is similar to the Catholic process, but Jews are encouraged to confess their sins during the penitential season of *Rosh Hashanah* and *Yom Kippur.*

## Yom Kippur

This holiday is our Day of Atonement, the most solemn of all Jewish holidays. It follows *Rosh Hashanah*, closing the penitential season. In Orthodox worship *Yom Kippur* is the day judgement is sealed upon us by the Heavenly Tribunal. But if the sinner repents and atones for his sin between *Rosh Hashanah* and *Yom Kippur* the judgement may be revoked, and so this is a day of at-one-ment with God through sincere repentance and nobler living. On *Yom*

*Kippur* Jews fast from sunset to sunset.

This most beautiful of ceremonies is begun with the singing by the *cantor* and congregation of the *Kol Nidre* (all the vows), the haunting and riveting song which petitions God to annul all vows, oaths and transgressions. My memory of hearing the *Kol Nidre* is with me even today. Its mournful tone and spiritual intensity make it impossible to hear without evoking strong emotion, even tears. If ever a song was made to reach the Supreme One, the *Kol Nidre* must be considered.

Even in biblical times Jews were in the habit of making many vows during emotional or perilous times which were impossible to keep, so a means had to be created whereby they could be released from them. These promises included those made during religious persecutions when Jews were forced to accept Christianity under duress. I remember a prayer during the afternoon service:

*O God, who is like unto Thee, that pardonest iniquity and passest by the transgression of the remnant of Thy heritage? Thou retainest not Thine anger forever, because Thou delightest in mercy...Union Prayer Book*

**Zion**

Zion to a Jew refers only to the land of Israel. Zionism is the reuniting of the Jewish people to their homeland, a task the *Mashiach* will be expected to accomplish. Living in *diaspora* Jews often turn in the direction of Israel when they pray.

# Bibliography

Clarification

In this book I have quoted from two bibles because I believe that process to be more representative of Hebrew history and language than other Bible printings. One Bible is the *Torah*, i.e. the Old Testament Bible which the Jews use, published by the Jewish Publication Society of America according to the Masoretic text. This translation has as its aim the incorporation of all the improvements which a large group of Hebrew scholars could give it. It tries to combine "the spirit of Jewish tradition with the results of biblical scholarship, ancient, medieval and modern." It carries with it, I believe, a spirit of Jewish consciousness.

Some quotations are followed by the words "Masoretic text." Though the differences between the Masoretic text and the King James version may seem small and restricted to differences in random words or short phrases, my intention is to represent Jewish thought, culture and history with whatever accuracy and insight is possible through the works which the Jews read and have always read. I invite my readers to compare scriptures, as I have done, and ask the Lord for a testimony of the truth.

This particular Masoretic translation follows Jewish tradition in that the texts are in three separate divisions: The Law (*Torah*), Prophets, Writings. Each section represents differing degrees of "holiness or authority," so that no book is translated into another. The books of Ruth, Lamentations and Daniel are all found in the Writings section instead of within the Prophets, where non-Jewish versions place them. These placements are thematically tied into the synagogue services where they are read.

I hope my perspective will enrich your own, that you will see in all this seeming disparity a potential unity.

Author's note

# Bibliography of Referenced Books

A Companion To Your Study of the Book of Mormon
Daniel H. Ludlow
Deseret Book, 1976
Salt Lake City, Utah

Answers to Gospel Questions, Volume 5
Joseph Fielding Smith
Deseret Book Company, 1966
Salt Lake City, Utah

The Articles of Faith
James E. Talmage
The Church of Jesus Christ of Latter-day Saints, 1982
Salt Lake City, Utah

The Book of Mormon, Another Testament of Jesus Christ
The Doctrine and Covenants
The Pearl of Great Price
The Church of Jesus Christ of Latter-day Saints, 1987
Salt Lake City, Utah

Book of Mormon Student Manual
Religion 121-122, Second Edition Revised 1981
The Church of Jesus Christ of Latter-day Saints,
Salt Lake City, Utah

The Complete Book of Jewish Observance
A Practical Manual for the Modern Jew
Leo Trepp
Behrman Books, Inc.Summit Books, 1980
New York

The Discourses of Brigham Young
Compiled by John A. Widtsoe
Deseret Book Company, 1954
Salt Lake City, Utah

The Holy Bible, King James Version
The Church of Jesus Christ of Latter-day Saints, 1987
Salt Lake City, Utah

The Holy Bible, Masoretic Text
Jewish Publication Society of America
Philadelphia  1985

Holy Mountain
Raphael H. Levine
WTS Publishing Company, 1962
Chicago

Invitation to the Talmud
A Teaching Book
Jacob Neusner
Harper & Row, 1973
New York

Jesus the Christ
James E. Talmage
The Church of Jesus Christ of Latter-day Saints, 1981
Salt Lake City, Utah

The Jewish Mourner's Book of Why
Alfred J. Kolatch
Jonathan David Publishing, Inc. 1993
Middle Village, NY

Jewish Wisdom
Rabbi Joseph Telushkin
William Morrow and Company, Inc. 1994
New York

The Joys of Yiddish
Leo Rosten
McGraw-Hill, 7th Printing 1976
New York, NY

*Les Miserables*
Victor Hugo
Fawcett Premier Book, 1961 edition
Greenwich, CT

Life Everlasting
Duane S. Crowther
Bookcraft, Inc. 1967
Salt Lake City, Utah

The Life and Teachings of Jesus and His Apostles
Course Manual, Second Edition
The Church of Jesus Christ of Latter-day Saints, 1979
Salt Lake City, Utah

The Mortal Messiah *from Bethlehem to Calvary*
Book One
Bruce R. McConkie
Deseret Book Company
Salt Lake City, Utah 1979

Scriptural Teachings of the Prophet Joseph Smith
Deseret Book, 1993
Salt Lake City, Utah

# <u>NOTES</u>

## About the Author

Marlena Tanya Muchnick was born in Canton, Ohio and raised in California, but is a devotee of the Pacific Northwest, though she does not like the rain! Baptized a Latter-day Saint April 6, 1988, Marlena has lived for many years in Oregon and Washington where she has served in the Church as a Stake missionary, Spiritual Living teacher, Gospel Essentials teacher and Relief Society coordinator. Recently returned from a full time mission in the Texas Houston Area, Marlena hopes to serve another mission eventually.

Marlena is currently finishing her second book, *Life Changing Testimonies of the Lord Jesus Christ*, to be published soon. A book of poetry is in the works. Marlena is currently working as a personal assistant to an orthopedic surgeon in the Seattle area. She invites all who are moved by her story to correspond with her ~~P.O. Box 725, Burton, Texas 77835~~. Her email address is:
For updates access: j

*Marlena Tanya Muchnick*
*LDS Author, Speaker*
*www.jewishconvert-lds.com*
*www.peopleofthebook.com*